Henry Collins

The Spirit and Mission of the Cistercian Order

Henry Collins

The Spirit and Mission of the Cistercian Order

ISBN/EAN: 9783744660273

Printed in Europe, USA, Canada, Australia, Japan

Cover: Foto ©Lupo / pixelio.de

More available books at **www.hansebooks.com**

THE SPIRIT AND MISSION

OF THE

CISTERCIAN ORDER:

COMPRISING THE LIFE OF

S. ROBERT OF NEWMINSTER,

AND THE LIFE OF

S. ROBERT OF KNARESBOROUGH;

WITH AN ACCOUNT OF THE FOUNDATION OF

FOUNTAINS ABBEY.

BY THE

REV. H. COLLINS, M.A.

"*Omnia Cistercium erat.*"

LONDON: SIMPKIN, MARSHALL & CO.
STATIONERS' HALL COURT.
DUBLIN: KELLY, GRAFTON STREET.
RIPON: HARRISON, MARKET PLACE.
1866.

TO

AMBROSE PHILLIPPS DE LISLE, ESQ.,

OF GARENDON, IN THE COUNTY OF LEICESTER,

FOUNDER OF ST MARY'S ABBEY,

OF MOUNT ST BERNARD,

IN THE FOREST OF CHARNWOOD,

OF THE PRIMITIVE OBSERVANCE OF THE CISTERCIAN ORDER,

THESE PAGES ARE INSCRIBED,

AS A TOKEN OF PERSONAL FRIENDSHIP,

AND OF GRATITUDE ON THE PART OF

A SON OF THE ORDER.

[THE historical part of this work is taken from ancient authentic documents; the mystical portions are principally from Görres' "Mystik." The history of S. Robert of Knaresborough is appended to that of S. Robert of Newminster, because many authors have supposed these two saints to be one and the same person, which is found to be a mistake.]

TABLE OF CHAPTERS.

S. ROBERT OF NEWMINSTER.

CHAP.		PAGE
I.	EARLY DAYS OF S. ROBERT—HE BECOMES A BENEDICTINE MONK,	5
II.	THE ERA IN WHICH S. ROBERT LIVED,	21
III.	WHAT TOOK PLACE AT S. MARY'S OF YORK,	34
IV.	FOUNDATION OF FOUNTAINS ABBEY—ROBERT ENTERS THE CISTERCIAN ORDER,	51
V.	THE CISTERCIAN IDEA,	67
VI.	INFLUENCE OF FOUNTAINS—FOUNDATION OF NEWMINSTER,	83
VII.	ROBERT'S LOVE OF SOULS—LIFE OF THE CLOISTER,	94
VIII.	THE PHILOSOPHY OF ASCETICISM,	108
IX.	MISSION OF THE CISTERCIAN ORDER,	121
X.	THE FRIENDS OF S. ROBERT—HIS DEATH AND ASSUMPTION TO BLISS,	135
XI.	DECADENCE OF THE CISTERCIAN ORDER,	147
XII.	PAST, PRESENT, AND FUTURE,	163

S. ROBERT OF KNARESBROUGH.

CHAP.		PAGE
I.	ROBERT'S CHILDHOOD—HE JOINS THE CISTERCIAN ORDER,	171
II.	ROBERT TURNS HERMIT — HIS CAVE AND CHAPEL AT KNARESBROUGH,	180
III.	ROBERT'S WAY OF LIFE—HE GOES TO SPOFFORTH — HIS VISION AND RETURN TO KNARESBROUGH,	187
IV.	ROBERT'S MIRACLES—VISIT OF KING JOHN—ROBERT'S DEATH AND BURIAL,	196

Ballantyne, Roberts, & Company, Printers, Edinburgh.

SPIRIT AND MISSION OF THE CISTERCIAN ORDER.

CHAPTER I.

EARLY DAYS OF S. ROBERT—HE BECOMES A BENEDICTINE MONK.

Light are their steps who in life's earliest dawn,
The mountain-tops of heavenly life ascend;
Brushing the dew-drops from the spangled lawn,
Nor ever from the straighter path descend;
Fixing their eyes upon their journey's end,
Sweetest, best thoughts are theirs, such as have striven,
With childhood and with dawning conscience blend,
To flee all other love but that of heaven,
Ere weighed to earth with sin and much to be forgiven.

GOD has His Saints in all ages. There are, however, some periods, when in greater prodigality He has bestowed these jewels on the world, out of the rich abundance of His treasures. But this mine of wealth is never exhausted. God contains within Himself an infinite number of these models of perfection; differing, indeed, in magnitude and lustre, as do the stars of the firmament. And as the stars are said to be shot forth from the sun to enlighten the darkness of the night, so does God send forth from the storehouse of His sanctity, these burning and shining lights to illuminate the shadowy gloom of this lower world. They came according to the decrees of His own blessed will; in some ages more, in other ages fewer. Happy is that age that can count them in the greatest number! The days when S. Robert lived were one of these happy favoured periods.

S. Robert was born at Gargrave, near Skipton, in Craven, in the diocese of York, towards the end of the eleventh century. He was, therefore, it would seem, about contemporary with the great S. Bernard. The exact date of his birth has not been handed down; but the circumstances of his life will hardly admit of any other time being fixed for it than the above. Neither the name nor the rank of his parents have been told us by the historians of his life. It is evident, however, from the education he received, and from what is said of his childhood, that they were persons of good station, and in easy circumstances as regards the things of this world.

To be born of parents endowed with a competent fortune, and to have thus the means of a liberal education, are advantages not to be slighted, or esteemed as nothing. It is true that by themselves neither worldly wealth nor high education are of any profit or value for the attainment of sanctity. God can, and sometimes does, make great Saints without them, as He did of the first apostles. These cases must, however, be deemed exceptions to the general rule of His providence. It was necessary that the first preachers should be unlearned and ignorant men, lest it might be said that the gospel owed its success to human wisdom, talents, and ability. But in His ordinary dealings with the soul, God is pleased to use the gifts of nature, and the accidental advantages arising from birth and education, as a stock on which to graft the more excellent things of grace.

Both the substratum and what is built upon it, though differing in their order and kind, are equally gifts of His beneficent hand.

Robert, we are told, was when a child very unlike what children usually are. At a very early age he showed predispositions for the kind of life, which he was called upon by God afterwards to embrace. He could find no pleasure in those games and diversions, which are usually so delightful a pastime to the young, and which seem suited to their years. He would therefore steal away from the companionship of his equals in age, and give himself to the exercise of holy prayer, or else to the reading and study of some sacred book. It was as if having determined that Robert's heart should be all His own, God jealously watched and guarded every avenue to it, for fear lest some worldly thing might enter to rob him of a portion of this treasure. David says to God of the just man: "Thou didst prevent him with the blessings of sweetness: Thou hast set a crown of precious stones upon his head." This crown of precious stones was for Robert, that circlet of graces and virtues to which God had destined he should attain. And in order that he might fall short in nothing, God was beforehand with the world; causing him to taste the blessings of His sweetness from his very infancy.

By this great grace, Robert escaped that which is the lot of most of the children of Adam,—the experimental knowledge of evil. Most even of the good are acquainted with two roads, the broad and the narrow way. Robert never knew but one. He could say with Job: "From my infancy piety grew up with me: it came out with me from my mother's womb." From his infancy he turned away his eyes from beholding vanity. Those eyes had already caught a sight of "the Land far off;" and ravished with its beauty, they refused to rest elsewhere. The world, doubtless, to him as to all others, held out the cup of its most sweet but deadly poison; but having tasted of the hidden manna and of the goodly wine mingled by wisdom, he loathed all other food. In vain was it for her to deck out her gilded baubles; and exert those charms, which she fancies invincible in order to bring him into captivity. She came too late. His heart was preoccupied; and he saw all with listless indifference, nay, with loathing aversion.

The dazzling tinsel bore no compare with the gold, clear as crystal, of his heavenly home. The best of her flowers soon faded; and having a right to the tree of life, he cared not for her choicest fruits. Diversions and amusements could be no real enticement to him, whose sweetest recreation was to be alone with God.

Thus was Robert a Saint when but a young boy. It has been said by one of the Fathers, that he knew more who had kept their robe of baptismal innocence unstained, than who had done worthy penance after sin. There is a deep mine of truth in this remark. There are comparatively few in the annals of the Saints, who have not been pious from their childhood. The impressions of grace received in childhood are of inestimable value to the soul—that season once gone by, and spent unprofitably, the graces thus forfeited can never be recovered. Other graces are to be obtained, it may be, but none like those, unless indeed by an extraordinary dispensation of God. S. Pachomius says, that in the heart of a child there is a special disposition for receiving the graces of God. Graces that take root in a child's heart are like plants set in a virgin soil. They grow up to a degree of perfection, majesty, and beauty, that under no other circumstances would have been attained. Our Lord's tomb was a new sepulchre, wherein never yet any man had been laid. And when He made His humble triumphant entry into Jerusalem, on the colt of an ass, He would have for this purpose one on which no man ever had sat. We may believe, then, that in like manner He takes a special delight in entering into the hearts of young children, whose freshness is yet unimpaired by the contaminating touch of the spirit of the world. Indeed, how can it be doubted that they have a special aptitude for His graces, and are in a particular manner dear to Him, when he Himself says, "Of such is the kingdom of heaven;" and adds, that if any one would enter into the kingdom of heaven, he must become like a little child. *We* are inclined to underrate children for the very reason for which He values them so highly. Our thoughts are very different from His thoughts. We look for something grand in external appearance and operation; and seeing nothing of this sort in children, we make little account of them. We look for a show of intellect, a great mind, and a brilliant display of talents. We see none of these things: and we forget what Jesus says, "I thank Thee, O Father, Lord of heaven and earth, because Thou hast hid these things from the wise and prudent, and hast revealed them to the little ones." The possession of those gifts, on which we set so much store, becomes indeed often a positive hindrance to the understanding of divine mysteries; and why? because those thus endowed are so prone to push the exercise of their intellect beyond the legitimate sphere of its operations. Even things supernatural must be subjected to its touchstone. This is the reason why even talented men have missed their road to truth, and wandered away into the basest delusions of folly. They have attempted by the insufficient light of mere natural reason, to judge of things altogether above its capacity, and with which it has no proportion. Those also who are conscious of having attained a certain amount of knowledge in spiritual things too often rest with pride on this acquired knowledge. And because they do not ask continually for fresh lights from the great Source of Light, they are punished with judicial blindness concerning the higher mysteries of the kingdom of God.

Children have no lofty thoughts of themselves. They have no need to make an act of humility. They are already little in their own eyes. They feel their own incapacity and weakness. A man of understanding, unless indeed he have retained a child-like spirit, has to bring himself down before God by a strong effort; his humility is, as it were, artificial. But a child in its artless simplicity, is already at that point to which he would fain bring himself by force. A child looks simply up to God: and the abyss of its littleness calls down the abyss of God's infinite greatness;—they meet and kiss one another.

Thus it is that a holy child has often views of God far clearer than have the most learned philosophers. These views come not by reasoning, meditation, or discourse, but by a simple view, a certain intuitive glance. Having no self-sufficiency, a child labours under no obstruction to its gazing upon God. God can communicate with it in freedom. He finds no obstacle to the revealing of Himself. This simple view, too, with which a holy child is gifted, is no mean possession, it is in kind, if not in degree, an exercise of exalted contemplation. The homage offered thus to God is of the purest nature. It is the 'clearest frankincense,' ordered by the old law to be burnt before Him. It is perfect praise. For the Holy Ghost does not say that God may be glorified in a measure even by children, but He calls their worship the perfection of praise: "Out of the mouths of babes and sucklings Thou hast perfected praise." Even those who turn to God after years of worldliness, negligence, folly, or sin, generally find the cause of their conversion in the good impressions of their childhood. These impressions were overlaid by evil habits; but had gone too deep to be rooted out. As for Robert, there is no reason to believe that he ever went astray from the path so early chosen. For him that saying of Solomon was true: "The path of the just is as a shining light, which shineth more and more until the perfect day."

There were in Robert's days few, if any, secular schools of learning. The Monasteries supplied their place, and it is most probable that his early education was confided to the tutelage of the Monks of some Benedictine Abbey. Whether in his boyhood he had ideas of devoting himself to God in the Religious life does not appear. It is probable he had not; for he seems to have been one of those characters who soon see their way to a conclusion, when the question is one of greater and closer union with God. It is true that, like Samuel of old, he had heard the voice of God speaking to him in the inmost depths of his heart, and asking for his love. He had answered also to the call: still it is not to be concluded from this, that when God first took possession of the heart given to Him, He therefore revealed all He intended to require.

The hill by which we mount towards heaven is, as it were, a winding path. The difficulties and length of the ascent are thus hidden partially from the view, and only what is soon to be required is made visible. It is thus that God would hide from faint-hearted and corrupted human nature the full extent of the sacrifices He intends to demand of it, lest it should in alarm shrink from the burden, as being utterly above its strength. Samuel when he first heard God's voice, did not know whose voice it was, but took it for that of Eli the priest. So when God first speaks to the soul, the soul often does not comprehend what is said, nor even feels assured that what she hears is truly the voice of God. She is not yet used to the sound. It comes to her like a vague murmur, or like a voice from a far-distant point coming over a mountain, and her ear, as it were, in vain endeavours to catch clearly the tone of Him who speaks. It is only by degrees, that as she advances the sounds become more distinct and articulate; just as in the case of Samuel, God came nearer after a while and spake plainly to him. It would seem, then, that God did not give to Robert as yet any distinct call to the Religious life. Having, however, a vocation for the ecclesiastical state, he passed successively through the various grades of the sacred ministry, and was ordained to the office of the priesthood. He was already remarkable on account of the great sanctity of his life, and, not content with that knowledge of the sciences and of theology which he could procure at home, he went to attend the schools at Paris, then the most celebrated for learning in all Christendom. Having good talents he made great progress, and was soon after his return made rector of his native village of Gargrave. Here he was brought more in contact with the world, and had to battle against the gross vices which then prevailed. M. Viannay, the curé of Ars, says he never knew the wickedness of the world till he learned its nature in the exercise of his ministry. This must be in a measure the case of almost all priests, but more especially of those who, from early childhood, have retained a remarkable purity of conscience. Whatever then might be the zeal of Robert for the spiritual welfare of his neighbours, we may be sure that the revelations he received of the world, in the discharge of his pastoral office, did not give it any more attractions in his eyes. It had nothing to offer him of value, but much to weary and disgust. His heart, therefore, went to and fro, like Noah's dove, finding no place to rest upon; and so it came to pass, that he determined to give himself to God with greater earnestness than ever; and to rivet himself fast in the chains of a love whose thraldom was as sweet as it was severe. This desire was to find its accomplishment in his embracing the call he now received to the religious life.

Happy are those souls whom God calls thus into the solitude, and whom He chooses to be His spouses. The world imagines that very great sacrifices must be made in order to follow a vocation to Religion. The world is deceived. Without doubt, one so called has to renounce what are termed enjoyments and pleasures, a name, family, relations, and friends. But for these trifles, abandoned for His sake, God gives compensation a hundred-fold above their value. The period of a man's entering into religion has been aptly called by S. Benedict, the time of his conversion. By the use of this term, it was not implied that all who entered a Monastery had been guilty at any time of following a lewd or vicious course of life. Far from it; for although this might not unfrequently be the case, it was by no means the rule.

But the term "conversion" is used, because the act of entering Religion implies a complete renouncement of all earthly things, to pursue those that are heavenly. There may, indeed, be said to be two kinds of conversion, an internal and an external.

The internal is the common property of all who are truly detached from the love of earthly things; whether they be in a Monastery, or are yet living in the world. For if they are in the world, they are in it but not of it. They have no relish for its enjoyments, but only for the things of the Spirit of God. The external is the act of entering Religion. This by itself is a mere shell; and, unless joined with an internal conversion of heart, is only useful so far as it lessens temptations, and disposes the heart for that internal conversion, which is the gate of the spiritual life, and the end and object of the Religious state.

But in order to comprehend what is meant by a man's conversion, some investigation must be made into the constitution of his being and his state since the Fall. Revelation, history, and the study of the things of nature, show us that the world, visible and invisible, is divided into, as it were, two kingdoms—darkness and light; and that man, placed between the two, is accessible to the influence of either the one or the other. Revelation tells us how this state of things came about. God having endued man with the knowledge of good at his creation, man added to it the knowledge of evil. From that moment there arose within him a terrible and incessant struggle. He bears within him two principles, so deeply seated as to saturate the very marrow of his being; the good principle he received from his Creator, and the evil with which he allowed himself to be inoculated by the devil. Thus he finds within him attractions to two opposite poles—a response for two voices. By the power of free will, and the assistance of grace, he is enabled to obey the higher attraction. Without the aid of grace he must have ever remained a slave to the lower; for since the Fall, man is become in a manner neutralised, the soul has become weak, and the body strong in proportion. All his relations to God, nature, and himself, have been turned upside down. The servant has become master; the exterior governs the interior. But when the soul is drawn to God by conversion, a complete revolution takes place in her sentiments and her powers. For to be converted is, instead of descending to things of nature, to ascend to those of God. The relations thus between man and nature are completely reversed. He begins to love what he hated; to hate what he loved.

Thus at his conversion he, in some sort, may be said to commence a new existence. The posture of his soul, the habitual direction of his thoughts and desires, is new. His whole life has, as it were, a new centre of gravity. He begins to reascend to that divine source of light and life, from communion with which the corruption of sin had separated him. It is God who takes the initiative in man's conversion by willing, in a positive manner, the return of the soul to Himself. Unless, however, the will of man concurs with this divine will, this union will never take place; and the divine will will be inefficacious in his behalf. God never gives so much grace as to force the will of man to comply. In His choice, however, and guidance of souls which He wishes to draw to Himself, God's action is alike independent of age, place, and circumstances, sickness or health. It disdains not the most simple, whilst it subjugates the loftiest intelligences. Even the state of the conscience is not decisive; for the perverse heart sometimes finds itself of a sudden broken by a stroke of grace and transformed, hardly knowing why or how. The action of God is the same in itself—the appearance of it differs according to the manner of its reception.

Thus the movement by which a soul is converted to God, seems sometimes slow and progressive; sometimes sudden, and like a stroke of lightning, according to His good pleasure and designs. When God takes possession of the soul, He announces his election by a certain warm breathing—an upward drawing, accompanied by an indescribable ray of light, which penetrates her through and through. Thenceforth the soul enters into a new life, under a special providence of His love.

This interior conversion of heart Robert seems to have possessed in his very childhood. It might seem to some that, if so, he required nothing more. But it was no doubt the very fact of his knowing the sweets of the divine communications of love, which made him long for some place where, without distraction, he might give his soul up to the embraces of his

He becomes a Benedictine Monk.

Divine Spouse. Besides, by a life of pious retreat, separated from the world, the powers of the soul are concentrated, and considerably augmented in energy, through the habit of recollection. It is in this way that the exterior conversion, and renouncement of the world, helps the interior, which ought always to accompany it. The discipline of the Religious life acts like a protecting shell to the tender fruit, and the continual exercises of piety minister to its nourishment and growth.

There was at this time at Whitby a Community of the Order of Clugni, living in great perfection, according to the reform of the Benedictine Rule introduced by S. Odo. Whitby, then called Streaneshalch, that is, bay of the lighthouse, had been formerly famous for the Monastery of S. Hilda, where the Abbot S. Wilfrid, afterwards Bishop of York, held a conference with the Scotch Bishop Coleman, A.D. 685, concerning the true time of keeping Easter. This Abbey had, however, been destroyed by the Danes. But in the time of William the Conqueror, William de Percie, ancestor of the Percies of Northumberland, rebuilt the Monastery, and gave it to the Benedictines. Here it was that Robert entered on the Religious life.

Richard, the third Abbot of the house, received the new postulant; and after the usual trial of a year, Robert, publicly in the oratory, pronounced his vow of obedience to him and his successors, according to the holy Rule of S. Benedict. Then having laid on the altar the schedule containing this written promise, thus calling to witness the Saints, whose relics were there deposited, he was professed, and clothed by the Abbot in the black habit of a Benedictine Monk. He was not destined, however, to remain here for life, as he no doubt supposed at the time of his profession. God had other designs for him; as will be seen in the sequel of his history.

CHAPTER II.

THE ERA IN WHICH S. ROBERT LIVED.

" What other yearning was the master tie
Of the Monastic Brotherhood, upon rock
Aerial,—or in green secluded vale;
One after one, collected from afar,
An undissolving fellowship? What but this
The universal instinct of repose,
The longing for confirmed tranquillity.
Inward and outward; humble and sublime,
The life where hope and memory are as one."
—EXCELSIOR.

IN order to arrive at a clear idea of the character of any man, great account ought to be made of the age in which he lived. Without this consideration, no fair estimate can be formed. There are certain dispositions and predispositions which each one inherits from his parents. Upon these greatly depends what he himself will be in after life. The education he receives, the circumstances into which he is thrown, and which are called fortuitous, all have their effect in moulding the character. It is true, no man can be properly called the creature of circumstances. Every man has a will of his own. If he had not, he would cease to be a responsible being. It would be unjust to punish him for evil conduct; and it would be equally unjust to reward him for doing well. The very fact that rewards and punishments have ever been the rule amongst mankind, is a proof that men have ever been regarded as responsible beings, and as having a free will of their own. It may be, therefore, laid down as a rule, even in matters of the divine order, that no man is ever condemned to eternal punishment without having first merited it. Having a true and veritable power of resisting temptation, he did not use the power.

Nevertheless, although this be perfectly true with regard to matters of salvation, namely, that the loss of a man's soul is caused by the evil use he has made of his free will, yet it is not true that the height of sanctity to which a man may attain, is equally dependent on his free will. All have salvation offered them freely. Here they may "buy without money and without price." But the highest seats in Christ's kingdom are not equally open to all. "To sit on my right hand and on my left, is not mine to give; but it shall be given to them for whom it is prepared of my Father."

There are peculiar graces given to some, which are never even offered to others. This it is which makes the Saints differ from others. Every one can be saved; but every one cannot attain the highest degree of sanctity. Doubtless, many might attain who never do, because many are called and few chosen; but many also live and die as ordinary good Christians, simply because they have never been called to anything else. "The preparations of the heart are from the Lord." He it is who there gives the interior call. For those who respond to the invitation, He prepares special graces, and He turns to account in their favour what we call the fortuitous circumstances of life, the age in which they live, &c., in order to bring them to that particular perfection of holiness which, from all eternity, He designed that they should reach.

The parentage, birth, and early years of S. Robert have been already spoken of; it remains to consider the age in which he lived, to the character of which he was in a measure conformed. That period was one of no ordinary stamp and character. It was an epoch big with importance both in Church and State.

During those days a sort of revolution passed over the people of Europe—the beginning of a new state of things. A thousand years had been spent in preparation for what then took place.

In the history of the Church, as in that of the world, there are certain periods, which to the eye of the observer stand out in a marked and distinct manner. It is because the things which have taken place in them are removed far above the common occurrences of her ordinary course. Such an eventful period was that great and glorious epoch, in which it was the lot of S. Robert to live. They were no ordinary times, but pregnant with mighty consequences to the future of Christendom. In his days a kind of spiritual revolution passed over the face of Europe, sweeping all before it.

Even common souls, when mixed up with a movement that is great and noble, are, by its contact, lifted up above themselves, and become great. S. Robert, however, was not merely to be one of those who are carried forward to great things by the inspiring influence of example; but he was to be one of the leaders of the onward movement; great above the great. But, before passing to any consideration of the events of this period, it will be best to go back to an early date, and to trace from thence the causes and the nature of this crisis.

Mystical theologians say that the soul, in her progress to perfection, passes through three stages. The first is called that of purgation; the second, of illumination; the third, of union. As it is with the individual Christian, so it may be said to be with the Church, in her corporate life: there are certain progressive stages on her road to perfection which, in analogy, answer to those through which each individual has to pass. Thus, the first ages are styled by Görres the purgative life of the Church. In those terrific persecutions which for three centuries spent their violence on the Church, and in the superhuman austerities of the first solitaries of the desert, we are presented with a lively picture of the persecutions of the world against every elect soul; and the self-abnegation she must exercise in the crucifixion of all natural pleasures.

It might be supposed, that when, in the reign of Constantine, the Christian religion obtained liberty of worship, her trials were at an end, her work of purgation completed. Alas! it was but at its beginning. It is true, the external violence of persecution was at an end; but on this very account, the interior purgation became the more difficult, by reason of the numbers of semi-heathen who crowded into her bosom. Whilst they became Christians in name, their hearts were but half-cleansed from the superstitions and moral corruption of Paganism. It was the prosperity of Christianity that gained their adhesion, rather than a love and admiration of her holy doctrines. It took, however, five centuries for Christianity to become the prevailing religion of the towns and cities; for, in the country, little had yet been achieved. The word "Pagan," according to its original signification, means a villager. We see from this expression how, long after the towns had been subdued, the villages and country places remained still sunk in their old superstition. What was done in the towns by the ministry of the secular clergy, was done afterwards for the country places by Monks and Nuns.

In A.D. 529 S. Benedict destroyed the Temple of

Apollo on Mount Cassino, where up to that time many idolaters used to gather together, and offer their abominable sacrifices. Here he founded the celebrated Monastery of Mount Cassino. His sister, S. Scolastica, presided over a Convent of women, not far distant. From thence they peopled Europe with their Monasteries. They generously adventured themselves into the forests of those countries, which were devastated by the barbarian hordes; and thus, after many a fluctuating conflict, they became victorious, and established Christianity wherever they went.

But alas! times of peace brought softness into the Monasteries. Under the temptation of riches and ease of life, the Rule of S. Benedict began to relax. When, therefore, the storm again arose—when the Lombards invaded Italy, the Saracens Spain—the north-east was desolated by the Normans, and the north-west by the Slavonians—when all was disorder, violence, and confusion—the Benedictines were found unequal to the struggle. They re-entered the world by whole troops, to live according to their desires. Matters were no better among the secular clergy. Simony and incontinence raged like a pestilential fever among their ranks.

The Religious Orders are the kernel of the Church. When they lose their fervour ruin begins to invade the whole body. Even the holy see itself was not exempt from being corrupted by the general demoralising spirit; and during the tenth century men very unworthy of the Papal dignity sat in the chair of S. Peter. In the very worst of times, however, evil never had it all its own way; and in proportion as the evil became worse, the opposition became more bold and strenuous. In the world, since the Fall, there has ever been, and ever will be to the end of time, this struggle between Esau and Jacob—between the flesh and the spirit. It is an irreconcilable enmity. And this opposition, of which every individual man has experience within himself, displays itself likewise in the fluctuation of society, and is reproduced from age to age; neither victory nor defeat being on either side ever complete. At certain times, however, the light gains signal victories and spreads its kingdom; going forth, as it were, to conquer the world and subdue it. It is, generally, when seemingly at the point of being overcome, that these achievements are wrought; just as it is ever darkest before the dawn of day.

The tenth century may be truly looked upon as the darkest and most unpromising period of the Church's history. It was in this age that God began to send forth those men, who were to rekindle in the Church that sacred fire, which seemed about to be utterly extinguished. In the year 910, S. Berno laid the foundation of the afterwards so celebrated Monastery of Clugni. Here the Rule of S. Benedict was carried out in all its strictness. S. Odo, who was then his disciple, became Abbot in 927. It was under his guidance that its influence began to extend far and wide through the Church—learning and piety began to flourish again, and the work of reformation to take root.

Another circumstance which must have had some influence in recalling Christians to the duties of their religion, was an idea which prevailed generally, that with the first thousand years after Christ, the world would come to an end. This anguished expectation finds its expression in the celebrated hymn, "Dies Iræ." The authorship of this hymn is ascribed to various persons, and its actual date unknown. It was not to be, as they expected, the end of the world, but it was truly the end of a certain state of things in the Church, and the commencement of a new period of a different character. After the first five hundred years of Christianity, a great decay of moral purity arose, which gradually spread, and burst like a flood, even into the sanctuary itself. The opposition to this evil became, however, gradually also more and more pronounced. It was only, however, in the eleventh century that it was anything like completely brought under. That century was the beginning of the illuminative life of the Church. It has been already mentioned how a prelude to the new state of things was made by the institution of the Monastery of Clugni. Here, after the death of S. Odo, S. Aymard, S. Mayeul, and S. Odilo were successively charged with the great work of reform. A few years later, S. Romuald, in 1009, founded the order of Camaldolese, still retaining the Rule of S. Benedict. In 1086, S. Bruno became founder of the Carthusians; and in 1098, S. Robert began at Molesme the Order afterwards called Cistercian. Thus a severe sanctity showed itself to the world in the Religious Orders; and in the beginning of the next century, 1126, the Order of Premontrè was added, by S. Norbert, to those already mentioned. The holy see also recovered its lustre, and ancient discipline revived. S. Leo, elected in 1049, eminently signalised himself in doing away with the abuses of the age; and S. Gregory VII., later on in the same century, carried on the reformation with unsparing vigour. But it was, in the providence of God, to the Cistercian Order principally that the completion of the work was to be intrusted.

As in the natural, so in the supernatural order, great changes are not wrought without considerable previous time for preparative steps. It is so in the individual man, it is so also in societies. The effectual change, too, is often preceded by impotent, unavailing efforts to bring it about. These ineffectual endeavours are not, however, so much loss, but form a necessary prelude to the acquisition of the desired object.

Mankind are not so many isolated atoms compacted together in order to form society, but they are in a manner parts of one body. There is an unseen electric chain, which binds together the human race, and which causes simultaneously a sympathetic movement between different individuals of the race — a movement which cannot be accounted for altogether by any merely external influence or impulses. The Cistercian movement was the climax of a revolt on the part of the nobler sentiments of man; a revolt against that softness, slothfulness, and barbarism, under the tyranny of which society had too long languished.

Even those who still allowed themselves to be held captive in these chains, felt with the movement. They could not but admire in sentiment what they had not the courage to imitate in practice. S. Robert, S. Alberic, and S. Stephen were men too much in advance of their age to do much. They had got before the vanguard of the advancing army. They and their followers were like a venturesome skirmishing band, whose heroic conduct was worthy of admiration, but who could not be expected to work in their own time any great results. They prepared the way by rousing the attention of society, and by giving cause for all hearts to burn within them, by the desire of better things.

It was through the instrumentality of S. Bernard, that the Cistercian spirit gained its wonderful sway. The extraordinary power possessed by this man of God, appeared first when he had determined to embrace the Religious life. He drew after him first his uncle, then his brothers, then his sisters, at last his father; and then the whole world went after him and became Cistercian. It was not precisely because of his talents, or his high position, that S. Bernard became the great man of his age. It may be with equal truth denied that his influence was due to the fact of his being the head of a rising and powerful Religious Order. Nor was it even his saintliness, great Saint as he was, that was the special cause and pivot of his power. Another Saint, though equal in sanctity, would not have been "S. Bernard," and would, consequently, not have had the same influence. It was not any one of these things taken in themselves; but it was because in the aggregate qualities and character of S. Bernard, the current age found embodied, in a living pattern, its ideas of excellence. In a religious point of view, this truly great epoch found its expression in the person of S. Bernard.

Before the death of S. Stephen, the great burden of the administration of the order devolved upon him. His Monastery of Clairvaux, which itself was an affiliation of Cîteaux, filled so rapidly, and so continuously, that it soon became a mother of many other houses, one hundred being founded by it in his own time. One of the earliest Cistercian houses in England was an offshoot of Clairvaux.

Under the reign of Henry, son of William the Conqueror, the kingdom of England enjoyed a profound peace; and new churches were erected every day by the piety of the faithful, to the great glory of God. Monasteries, also, were built on every side; and religion extended itself, and struck its roots deeper into the hearts of the people. To this king the holy Abbot wrote a letter, sending with it a colony of his Monks, to whom he had given his secretary William for Abbot. He told the king in his letter that his children were come into England, hoping to find some place there where they might in quiet serve God and the kingdom of Jesus Christ. He recommended them to the king's care, praying him to give them all the assistance of which they might stand in need.

They were received by this prince and all the nobles of his court with great honour; and thence retiring into the diocese of York, they laid the foundation of the celebrated Abbey of Rievaux. This was the first house of the Cistercian Order in that diocese, and the second founded in England.

The Monks that formed this colony were men of eminent virtue and piety. They gloried, says the historian, in their poverty and humiliations, and were at peace with all, saving their own bodies and the common enemy of men. With the strictest exactitude they observed the discipline they had learned at Clairvaux; and the sweet odour of their virtues was shed abroad on all sides like a precious perfume. Quickly the news spread throughout the adjacent parts of the country, that there had arrived men whose sanctity was so great, and their life so austere, that they were rather angels living on earth than mere men. Many felt impelled, by the inspirations of grace, to become imitators of their holiness, so that in a short time their number was very much increased.

CHAPTER III.

WHAT TOOK PLACE AT S. MARY'S OF YORK.

> *" Try not the pass," the old man said;*
> *" Dark lowers the tempest overhead,*
> *The roaring torrent is deep and wide."*
> *And loud that clarion voice replied,*
> *" Excelsior!"*
> —LONGFELLOW.

ROBERT we left at Whitby Abbey, following the Benedictine Rule according to the reform of Clugni. The examples of piety and sanctity at Rievaux were not without their effect on him. He had, indeed, for some time before felt a great longing for a more austere life than that practised in the Clugniac Monasteries. God, who had inspired him with these desires, brought them to effect in the following manner:—

There were, in the Abbey of S. Mary's of York, certain Monks who, following the customs received from their fathers, lived in great piety according to the Rule of S. Benedict. It must, however, be allowed that they did not follow that Rule with anything like the exactitude of the new Cistercian Order. It came to pass, therefore, that on the fame of Rievaux coming to their ears, some of them felt much pricked in their conscience, as though they bore the name of Monks without having the true spirit of their state. The imperfection with which they kept the Rule appeared, by the side of the mortified lives of the Monks of Rievaux, to their great disadvantage. Negligences, formerly indulged in without scruple, on a sudden took the appearance of glaring infractions of the Rule and sins against their vows. They were seized with fear and remorse, and thought that salvation would be impossible for them, unless by worthy penance they should wipe off those sinful relaxations which they had allowed themselves. They were weary of their lukewarm life, and felt quite confused to think of the soft unworthy manner of carrying out their holy profession. Tired of the noise of the city and the worldly tumult around them, they sighed with ardour for some lonely unfrequented place, some solitude, where they might work with their hands for their daily bread, content with the coarsest food that could supply their necessities.

Those who thus united together to consecrate themselves to a life of real penitence, were seven in number—Richard the Sacristan, Ralph, Gamel, Gregory, Hannon, Thomas, and Gaultier. In order to succeed in their design the better, they at first intended to keep secret their resolution of seeking a new kind of life. This was for fear it might come to the knowledge of Richard the Prior. For Richard being in high favour with the great men of the kingdom, and much esteemed by the Archbishop of York, might easily overthrow all their projects. Nevertheless, after a while, seeing that sooner or later the affair must be brought before him, they took the resolution of revealing to him the troubles of their conscience, together with the designs they entertained of leading a stricter life. Accordingly, they went one day to him, and opened to him the whole matter; begging him also to give his assistance in furthering the object of their desires. Richard was taken quite by surprise. Nevertheless, when he had well considered all that was said, he not only consented to further their proposition, but even promised that he himself would be one of them; giving great thanks to God for inspiring them with such holy dispositions.

The consent of Richard to their project, caused to these good Monks inexpressible joy and consolation. Now they could speak of the matter with more freedom: animating one another to firmness in their purpose, and striving also to gain over some others of their brethren. At last the number mounted up to thirteen, among whom was Gervais, the Sub-prior. These unanimously came to a resolution to put themselves under the Order of Cîteaux, in order that they might follow out the entire Rule of S. Benedict. Without further delay they debate among themselves as to what plan they must pursue, so as to succeed in getting away from their Abbey. The idea of poverty caused them no fear, nor the rigour of the frost and cold of the coming winter. They thought only of how their desire might be accomplished without giving cause of trouble or scandal to others.

This was indeed a very difficult matter. The report soon spread through the Abbey that Richard the Prior, and some others with him, were being carried away by a spirit of inconstancy; that they had a design of separating themselves from their brethren, with a foolish idea of seeking greater perfection, to the disgrace of their house, and indeed of the whole Order. They were accused and condemned for fickleness and indiscretion; as breakers of order, and disturbers of the peace of the Monastery. Their conduct was esteemed as a violation of their vow, a rupture of brotherly charity, an open contempt of the ordinances of their Fathers, and altogether scandalous. The whole Abbey became filled with confusion and tumult. All the brethren opposed the enterprise, as a piece of temerity worthy of severe punishment, proceeding from pride and a contempt of their seniors.

Things were in this state when Richard the Prior, taking with him the Sub-prior Gervais, a man highly esteemed in the Abbey on account of his great virtue, went to seek Geoffrey, the Abbot. This was on the vigil of the Feast of S.S. Peter and Paul 1132. Arrived in his presence, they open to him their whole heart, hiding nothing.

The Abbot was a man far advanced in years, simple and illiterate, but a really good man. When he had learned from the Prior the errand on which they had come, surprise, grief, and indignation, in a mingled tide, took possession of his soul. He deplored his unhappy lot, that at his age such a misfortune should come upon him. He was inconsolable for the shame that would thus be brought on the house; the upsetting of his Community and the loss to his Order. He implored them, therefore, to give up the thought of so pernicious an enterprise, one so full of presumption;—to remember that, by their solemn profession they were now no longer at their own disposal, and that they never could break the agreement they had made before God's altar. He threatened to treat them with that severity with which the Order punished apostates: in a word, he declared he would never permit them to leave the Monastery, nor would he change the ancient customs observed by his Order throughout the world. The Prior having listened with the respect that was due to his Abbot, then made the following reply:—

"We have no desire, Reverend Father, to introduce any extraordinary things or new customs into the house. We are, as it is, under the obligation of observing, with all the fidelity we are able, those holy and ancient practices which in his Rule our Father

S. Benedict prescribes to us, or rather which the Gospel, more ancient than all Rules, has ordained. We think that no one ought to be offended at the design we entertain of reforming our manners and conduct. We judge no one else, nor condemn their customs. We know that in every place Jesus Christ is served as the one only sovereign Lord, and that all fight under the standard of this King of kings. We know that in public places, as well as in the cloister, God can make the power of His grace to shine forth, as may be seen by the example of Job, who was more powerful when seated on a dunghill than Adam in the midst of paradise. In fine, Reverend Father, all that S. Benedict has established in his Rule is so plainly the work of the Holy Ghost, that nothing can be conceived more profitable, more holy, or more desirable.

"As he knew that idleness is the enemy of the soul, he laid down certain times for reading, for prayer, and for working with the hands, in order that in reading and prayer the soul might find her proper food; and, on the other hand, the body being exercised in labour, the Monks might have all their moments so occupied as never to fall into sloth, nor become a prey to weariness and disgust." In another place he says—"As for jesting and idle words, and such as move to laughter, we condemn them to eternal exclusion from all places of the Monastery, and permit not the disciple to open his mouth for the utterance of such words," and in another place, "the Monks ought at all times to keep silence, but particularly during the hours of the night." Nevertheless, who is ignorant how little we observe these precepts? for whilst some go to the church at the close of the reading before Compline, others, on the contrary, get together and amuse themselves with idle and trifling discourse. As if the day were not enough for such disorders, the night must be added also.

After making certain remarks about excess in eating and drinking, and in the use of fine and costly stuff for wearing apparel, he continued,—"These things are not according to the sentiments of our Father S. Benedict. He has no regard to the colour,* but only to the warmth, of what is to be worn. He wishes us in our food not to seek to please the palate, but to satisfy necessity, and he holds for his disciples those only, who, besides being subject to an Abbot, are obedient also to the Rule."

Richard then enlarged on the cupidity with which wealth was sought after by the Clugniac Monks, noting how little in this and other matters the Gospel rules were adhered to.

He then went on to say—"If we find the precepts of the Gospel too high for us, let us cast our eyes on the Monks of Savigni and of Clairvaux, who not long since have arrived in these countries; and we shall

* The Cistercian habit was of undyed wool, dyes being esteemed luxurious, because expensive, in the Middle Ages.

see that they practise what is contained in the Gospel with such perfection, that if one may so speak, it is of more profit to look at their lives than to read the Gospel. For if one regard the sanctity of their lives, they seem like a living representation of the Gospel; so that if the book were lost, it would suffice to behold them, to know what it teaches. They alone do not ask back what is their own: they alone possess nothing to give them the advantage over others. They are content with a few fields, which they cultivate themselves, for a small number of cattle which they use. Even these things they only desire as long as it may please God to give them; and if deprived of them, they would not demand them back, however just their cause might be. They can truly say with the apostle: 'The world is crucified to us, and we to the world.' 'Forgive us our offences and our debts, for we forgive those who have offended against us, and who are indebted to us,' for they do not exact of their debtors what they owe. Monks like these are, indeed, something great and admirable; how happy are they. There is nothing in them, nor in their manner of life, which has not a perfume of the Gospel about it. God alone is their heritage, and they desire nothing else besides Him.

"They indeed love God and their neighbour, in as perfect a manner as can be done by men; for, attaching themselves to God alone, they have made an absolute renunciation of all the things of this life;

being content with the poor vile habit they wear, and possessing nothing which can draw on them the eyes of the envious. Do not think then, Reverend Father, that it is impossible to observe the Rule of S. Benedict, when we have before our eyes such examples. If indeed the neighbourhood and tumult of the world in which we live, hinder us from following the height of perfection in all things, at least let us render our lives comfortable to our Rule; for, to speak the truth, we are dead persons rather than living Monks. '*Non monachi, sed mortui sumus.*'"

Such in effect was Richard's answer: the Abbot was not satisfied. It is very difficult to change customs to which we have been habituated. However, after having said for himself that he had not sufficient light and knowledge to judge of the matter, he begged Richard to put down in writing all that he had in his thoughts, which Richard willingly promised to do. A memorial, therefore, was drawn up by him. In this he marked out how he thought things ought to be regulated, whether with regard to their conversations, their food, clothing, manual work, &c. He added also, that what revenues and tithes they possessed, with the permission of the Bishop, should be devoted to the sustenance of poor persons, guests, and strangers.

When the other Monks learned the contents of this memorial, they were exceedingly exasperated against the Prior, declaring that he and his party ought to be expelled from the Monastery. The Abbot was, however, more moderate; and after several conversations on the subject, he replied at last, that it was a difficult thing to change the customs of his predecessors; that he would take advice on the matter, and would put off any final decision till the Feast of the Nativity of the Blessed Virgin.

The other Monks were fearful of being obliged to lead a more strict life; and they, therefore, began to persecute the Prior, or at least to endeavour to get some power so to do. At last rumours of what was going on got outside, and came to the ears of Thurstin, the Archbishop of York, a wise and discreet prelate. The rumours were only of a confused nature; but later on the Prior, Sub-prior, and Richard the Sacristan, sought an interview with him, and opened to him the whole state of the case. The Prior was the spokesman of the three. He told the Archbishop what he conceived the Rule of S. Benedict required, and how their life hitherto had been anything but exact to the Rule, which they had vowed to take for their guide. He spoke of the remorse they felt on account of their want of strictness, the vehement desires they entertained of rising to a better and more perfect way of life. He then mentioned the opposition on the part of some of the Monks, the prohibitions of the Abbot, the threats of expulsion. In fine, he begged humbly for the protection and patronage of the Archbishop; that he would mercifully take them under his wing, and assist them in their resolution to carry out their enterprise and desires. He besought him also to give that assistance promptly, because some of their number, for fear of giving offence, and out of old friendship, were beginning to falter in their purpose, and, if there were any delay, might altogether fall from it.

The Archbishop, having well considered the matter, could not doubt but that the project of Richard was the design of the Right Hand of the Most High. Giving thanks, therefore, to God for His graces, and conceiving it was his duty to further, as far as lay in his power, the accomplishment of so holy a purpose, he first consulted with divers persons how he might best act in the matter. He then endeavoured, by sending a message to the Abbot, to get the affair peaceably settled. The Abbot, however, gave his final answer, that though not personally opposed to a more perfect carrying out of the Rule, he could not introduce any difference in its observance without the consent of the other Monks. That consent was not to be had. This result being reported to the Archbishop, he appointed a day, the sixth of October 1132, for the visitation of the Abbey.

When the Abbot received word of the intended visitation, fearing lest the Archbishop should favour those Monks who wished to quit the Abbey, he sent to the different Clugniac Monasteries for the most learned and able of their body, intending, through their influence and authority, to withstand anything that the Archbishop might be inclined to do in favour of those Monks who desired to lead a more strict life. Amongst these champions of the Clugniac Benedictines, came Robert, as the representative of Whitby Abbey. This was a special providence of God in his behalf, for it afforded him an occasion of embracing that stricter life, which he had already so longed after. He had been called upon to oppose the innovators; and when he arrived he found that in spirit he was already on their side. In their desires he saw nothing but the reflection of those he had long entertained in his own breast. As iron sharpens iron, the hearing of their desires made his own more keen. The sight of the Monks themselves, the being in their company, was an incitement to join their holy undertaking. A life of silence and of solitude—a life of penance and privation—of poverty and austere discipline;—this was just the thing he had pictured out to himself. He saw, therefore, in their proceedings no innovation at all, but only the purpose of living in accordance with that Rule, which had so long in name been their guide. What could be more reasonable than, as Benedictines, to wish to follow the course laid down for them by their holy legislator? These were the workings in his mind, of which the result was soon to become manifest.

On the morning of the sixth of October, as already arranged, the Archbishop came to the Abbey to make his formal visitation, in order to try and settle the matter in a peaceable manner. He was accompanied by a few of his Clergy, Canons, and Religious, to the number of seven persons. The Abbot, attended by a number of Monks from all parts of the country, met him at the door of the Chapter-House, and forbade the entry of any of those who accompanied the Archbishop, saying that secular clergy ought not be made a party in the affairs of their Chapter, for fear of overturning the discipline of the Order. If the Archbishop would enter, he must do so alone. The Archbishop replied, that such a course was not befitting his dignity and office; and that he could not send away those very persons whom, on account of their wisdom and high standing, he had brought with him to afford him their advice; and the more especially, when he saw on the side of the Abbot so many Monks, not belonging to his Abbey, but strangers from all parts of the country. When the Archbishop had spoken, the Clergy who were with him tried to force their way into the Chapter. The Monks, on the contrary, opposed them, each disputing with the other at the same time—the one party demanding entrance, and the other refusing, in loud tones. The Archbishop, however, commanded silence, and said: "God is our witness that we came hither with the affection and charity of a father, thinking no evil, but desiring to bring you to peace one with another. But seeing that you do this day withdraw the obedience due to us, we, by the authority of God, withdrawing that power which ye have from us, do interdict this Church; and we suspend the Monks of this Abbey from the exercise of all sacred functions." When he said this, one of the Monks named Simeon cried out, "Well, let our Church be interdicted; we had rather it were so for a hundred years, than see you enter our Chapter."

The Prior and those with him, fearing to remain any longer in the house, implored the Archbishop to take them away with him, which he kindly consented to do. He then retired with the Prior and the other twelve Monks into the Church, probably his Cathedral, and from thence to the Bishop's palace.

Nevertheless, Abbot Geoffrey left no stone unturned in his endeavours to get his Monks back. He wrote a complaint to the King; and, besides that, to the Bishops, Abbots, and persons of piety in the realm, representing them as apostates, deserters, traitors, &c. He succeeded in getting two to return, Gervais, the Sub-prior, and Radulph; Gervais, however, subsequently repented, and again joined the seceders. Their number, in all, was now twelve. The rebellion of the Monks against their Archbishop greatly scandalised Robert, and thus prepared the road for his withdrawal from those who had been guilty of such a misdemeanour. The new colony waited the issue of affairs in the Archbishop's palace. Thurstin took care to write to William, Archbishop of Canterbury, the Pope's legate, an account of the whole affair, in order that he might not be gained over to credit the slanders of the opposing party. He concludes his letter in the following terms :—"We entreat, therefore, your fatherly goodness to take their part, and by your authority to defend those who are desirous of embracing a more strict and austere life. If their Abbot come to you, according to the wisdom and authority given you by God, send him away in peace, and warn him not to impede the holy design of his sons. If he has already been, and is departed, we ask you to direct to him letters by our messenger; telling him not to oppose, but rather to assist, these men, who desire in very deed to obey the Gospel of Christ, and the Rule of the blessed Benedict. And they are not to be considered deserters, who, leaving a place where there is liberty of offending, wish to serve God with more safety. In the conferences of the Fathers, the hermit Joseph teaches plainly enough, that he who betakes himself to a place where he may more fully carry out the precepts of the Lord, keeps thus with more rectitude the faith of his profession.

"Nevertheless, in consideration of the weak, who do not know the truth, we entreat your Holiness to endeavour to restore peace between the aforesaid brethren and their Abbot. Lastly, we should remember a similar colony of Monks of Molesme first instituted and founded the most perfect Rule of the Cistercian life, which the whole Church admires; whose purity the Lord Archbishop of Lyons, of venerable memory, has with Christian piety so praised. And, when complaints of the envious came to the Apostolic See, a decree was given by Urban II., the Pope, that "the Abbot alone, being restored, is to rule over his Abbey; of the rest of the Monks none shall suffer hindrance or be troubled, if he wish to persevere in the full observance of the Rule."

The Abbot Geoffrey thought of gaining over S. Bernard to his side, and obtaining the interference of the latter on his behalf. He therefore wrote to him, representing the grief of his heart, the troubles of his old age, the scandal to his Monastery and his Order, occasioned by the secession of this band of Monks. He gained, however, nothing; for S. Bernard defended the seceders, saying, that to return would be an apostasy. Geoffrey wrote again, asking his reasons for so saying, and S. Bernard replies, after some other remarks: "You demand earnestly why they should deserve the appellation of apostates if they return to your Monastery, and study with a good way of life to fulfil their profession. I, I say, would not condemn them. The Lord knoweth them that are His; and let every one bear his own burden. For the Lord, whom the darkness comprehendeth not, shall be known when He maketh judgment; and the sinner shall be taken in the works of His own hands. Let each one think as may please him; for myself, I will say what I think. If I, Bernard, had passed from good to better,—from danger to security—freely in will and deed, should have presumed, by an unlawful will, to return to what I had altered from,

I should be in fear, not only of becoming thus an apostate, but also of not being fit for the kingdom of God. This also the Blessed Gregory says : 'Whoever has purposed to strive after a greater good, the lesser good, which was lawful, he has made unlawful; for it is written : "No man, putting his hand to the plough, and looking back, is fit for the kingdom of God."' But he who was determined on a nobler course, is convicted of looking back, if he returns to lesser goods, leaving those of greater excellence. As to the excommunication you would interpose, it seems to me to be neither your interest to be over-diligent, nor mine to judge in such a matter. The law judges no man except he first be heard. To pass judgment on the absent is a rash proceeding."

CHAPTER IV.

FOUNDATION OF FOUNTAINS ABBEY—ROBERT ENTERS THE CISTERCIAN ORDER.

> *" It was a barren scene and wild,*
> *Where naked cliffs were rudely piled;*
> *But ever and anon between*
> *Lay softest tufts of loveliest green;*
> *And well the Monk or Hermit knew*
> *Recesses where the wall-flower grew:*
> *He deemed such nooks the sweetest shade*
> *The Sun in all its rounds surveyed."*

TWO months and a half were thus passed in the Archbishop's palace; and as there was now a full prospect of the Monks being left to follow their vocation without being further molested, the Archbishop looked out for some place where he might settle this new colony, where they might be at liberty to build their Monastery, and give themselves up to their austere life without hindrance.

In December the Archbishop went with his attendants to celebrate the Feast of Christmas at Ripon. About three miles from thence was a place called Skell-dale, in the Patrimony of his Cathedral of S.

Peter. This place he assigned as a settlement for the Monks; adding afterwards to this gift the village and land of Sutton, in its neighbourhood. This dell was at that time a most inhospitable place; more proper as a retreat for wild beasts than a suitable abode for mankind. It was all overgrown with thorns, briers, and brushwood; situated among rude and jagged pieces of rock, which formed cliffs on all sides. Here, then, was the commencement made of the afterwards so famous Fountains Abbey. Whether this name "Fountains" was conferred on it in honour of the name of S. Bernard's birthplace, "Fontaines," a town of Burgundy, or arose from the Monks being accustomed to latinise the Saxon word "Skel," (a fountain,) cannot be determined with certainty.

Having taken possession of this place with all those legal forms that were necessary to secure to them an undisturbed right, they then proceeded to the election of an Abbot. Their choice unanimously fell on Richard, the ex-Prior of S. Mary's of York. The Archbishop presided at the election, and invested the Abbot-elect with the full authority for the discharge of his office, by bestowing on him the usual Abbatial Benediction. S. John's Day, December 27, 1132, was the day on which the foundation of Fountains Abbey was laid. But what were these poor Monks to do? They had no place where to lay their heads, and the season was the middle of winter. Certainly it required a stout heart to brave all the difficulties of their situation! The cold of an English winter is a very severe thing, on account of the damp nature of the climate; though, as far as the thermometer goes, the frost in other countries may be more severe.

Besides having to defend themselves from the cold, the rain and melting snow were other enemies with which it was hard to deal; and in all their extremities they found themselves without money, without provisions, or even the very necessaries of life; except so far as the charity of the Archbishop might purvey to their wants. The shelter of the rocks was at first their only protection against the cold, which at night was very piercing. It was some relief when, finding a large elm in the middle of the vale, they threw over its spreading branches a covering of thatch, as some shelter from the inclemency of the weather. Against the searching winds, they erected a tent-work with some pieces of blanketing given them by the Archbishop. It was a poor shift! but they could do no better. This formed their dormitory. They there slept together beneath the tree—eleven priests and one sub-deacon. Thurstin supplied them with bread, and the skell with water. At night they rose for Vigils, and sang them in the manner ordained by the Rule of S. Benedict.

They applied themselves with great fervour to prayer and recollection, animating each the other by their holy examples. By day they laboured in the construction of an Oratory, cutting down the trees of the surrounding forest for this purpose. Others again busied themselves in laying out a garden, breaking up the ground, and preparing it for the reception of seed.

They did not eat their bread in idleness; but though the meal was but a scanty one, it was not till after they had been worn out with fatigue that they tasted it. There was, however, no sound of a murmur to disturb the peace and tranquillity that filled the breasts of these solitaries. No sadness could reach them, whose joy did not consist in the abundance of possessions, but was that of the Holy Ghost, which the world can neither give nor take away. Before the winter was over, it is supposed they changed their elm for a shelter of seven yew trees, six of which are now standing on the south side of the ruins of the Abbey. Such is the tradition; and when it is considered how little a yew-tree increases in a year, and to what an amazing bulk these are grown, the tradition seems probable. The side of the hill was covered with wood, which is now almost all cut down. It looks, therefore, as if these trees were left standing to perpetuate the memory of the Monks' habitation under their cover, during the first winter of their residence.

Robert had returned to Whitby after the events related in the last chapter, which took place at S. Mary's Abbey of York. Here he waited till he might see how matters should turn out. When, however, he heard that the emigrants were now provided with a settlement, unfurnished though it was, and though it was the depth of an English winter, he asked and obtained leave of his Abbot to go and join them. Oh! these were the days when men dared much, because they loved much. These men seem to have practised, to the letter almost, that saying of S. Bernard's, that whoever knocked at the gates of his Monastery must leave his body outside; and his spirit alone must enter. That life must indeed have been an ecstatic life, which could exalt its possessors so far above the ordinary course of nature's wants, that in the middle of winter, a season so inhospitable in England, men should, without any other shelter than the rocks, the forest trees, and the brushwood, go forth to commence the building of their new home. Robert, if prudent, as the world counts prudence, would have waited a while, but he feared to be robbed of any part of his share in the hardships of the first foundation. He therefore hastened to make use of the permission he had obtained, and bidding farewell to his Benedictine Brethren, started for Fountains, and found them hewing down trees for the building of the Oratory. His coming was a great consolation to them; and he soon showed that he was no way behind hand in the zeal with which he embraced the new kind of life, for, to speak the very truth, whether in labours of the hands, in watchings or fastings, or whatsoever else it might be which they practised, he fairly outdid them all.

This, then, was Robert's first taste of the Cistercian life. Had he shrunk from the chalice God held out to him;—had he turned aside from the thorny path, —he might have had, indeed, a sweeter cup in the things of this life—a less painful road on which to tread, but oh, what forfeits in the Day of the Resurrection!

The winter being over, the young Community held a consultation as to the best manner of observing their Rule, and as to whether they had not best apply to S. Bernard, to be received into the Order of Cîteaux. After some consideration, this appeared to them the best course. For, in the first place, it would free them from the responsibility of being their own guides; and, furthermore, it would save them a world of distraction and perplexity in providing regulations for such points as are not sufficiently legislated for by the Rule itself.

Without further delay they sent messengers to Clairvaux, asking to be received into the Order of Cîteaux, and promising to give filial obedience in all things.

Thurstin wrote also to S. Bernard, recommending them to his charity, and confirming the account they gave of themselves in their letter to the Saint. The messengers, having arrived at Clairvaux, were received with greatest kindness, and the utmost sympathy of brotherly love was shown towards them.

After having kept them a short time at Clairvaux,

where they were filled with joy and edification at what they saw, S. Bernard sent them away, carrying with them a letter to the Community, and one to the Archbishop. The letter to the Community runs in the following quaint terms:—"As we have heard so have we known, and our Brethren, the two Geoffreys, have told us, how ye are warmed anew with the fire of God; ye are recovered from sickness; ye have flourished again in holy newness. This is the finger of God, working with subtilty, sweetly renovating, healthfully changing; not making the bad good, but the good better. Oh that I might pass over and see this great sight! For the advance from good to better is no less admirable than the change from bad to good. Indeed, it were more easy to find many men of the world converted to good than one Religious passing from good to better. He is a '*rarissima avis in terris*' who ascends a little above the degree he had attained in Religion. Deservedly, then, does your deed, both honourable and advantageous, make glad, not us only, but the whole city of God."

To the Archbishop he wrote:—" Even before this, all the Church of the Saints told of your alms; but this was a thing common to many, since all are obliged to give of their substance. But for this bishoply action—this excellent specimen of your fatherly affection—this truly divine fervour, with which, for the protection of the poor, He who maketh His angels Spirits, and His ministers a burning fire, has lighted up your zeal,—this work is special to you, a glory of your dignity, the ensign of your office, the ornament of your crown."

S. Bernard sent back with the messengers his secretary Geoffrey. Geoffrey of Amaie was a man now far advanced in age, a man of rare piety, and one of singular modesty and gravity. He had a deep and vast knowledge of things, both human and divine; and S. Bernard had often made use of his services in the foundation of various Monasteries. Being arrived at Fountains, he was received with the honour he deserved, and his presence was a great consolation to the Brethren. They begged without further delay to be instructed in the Cistercian manner of living; assuring him that to be under the discipline of S. Bernard, was to them a matter of the very greatest joy. Following his advice, they erected simple and small buildings, arranged the places for labour, and, in a word, embraced with an exact fidelity all the ways of the Order of Cîteaux.

One of the things Geoffrey was specially commissioned to do, was to teach them the Cistercian method of Chant. The solemn performance of "the work of God," as it is styled by S. Benedict, had great attention paid to it by the first Cistercians. "With such solemnity and devotion do they celebrate the Divine Office," says Stephen of Tournay, "that you might fancy Angels' voices were heard in their concert." There was nothing of artificial ornament to set off their

Chant. It was but the simple grandeur, and unaffected majesty of the old Gregorian melodies sung in unison, which had such effect.

As in other things, so in their music they were declared enemies to all that was not plain and simple. In their choirs was to be heard no stentorian clamour, no soft or effeminate trillings, no quaverings or affected tremulousness of the voice, no falsetto. The Chant was ordered to be neither high nor low, neither precipitate nor trailing, the voice being given full and round, with all moderation, so that none should be heard above the others, but all might march together, in equal sound and with equal pace. On great Festivals the Chant was slow and solemn, and the pauses long, but not so as to inspire tedium. On common days it was sung with more briskness, yet still without hurry.

The music of the Church had suffered much during the decay of discipline in the Monastic Orders. It became one of the chief cares of the Cistercian Rule to rectify the disorders that had crept into the Church's Song, and to correct the meretricious style, which had been introduced not only into Cathedrals and Parish Churches but even into Monasteries. The Liturgical Books underwent a strict revision, and all modern innovations were extirpated without mercy. With all its plain simplicity the Cistercian mode of chanting won the admiration of the age. Its effect was peculiarly touching, drawing to compunction even the hardest hearts. This, indeed, was its object and aim, for they sought not by their strains to tickle the ear, but rather to kindle in themselves, and in the breasts of all who heard them, the flames of divine charity. Unfortunately the evil spirit of the Pagan Renaissance found its way in process of time even into the cloistered solitudes of the Cistercian Abbeys. There, under pretence of classical reform, it committed sad havoc amongst the Psalters and Antiphonaries of S. Bernard and S. Stephen. With its mutilating knife it cut away the magnificent luxuriance of the old Cistercian Song, robbing it at the same time of its grave and stately majesty by an attempt to square all with the rigid rules of prosody. It is to be hoped that in these days of Christian revival a new edition of the Cistercian Chants may be published, not formed after the corrupted version of modern times, but an edition of the authentic melodies, as they stand in the Liturgical Books of the Order in the days of its glory.

Geoffrey was in admiration at the obedience, poverty, mortification, and temperance of the new disciples of Cîteaux. Yet with all their hardships, they had scarcely commenced, when God sent them ten Novices, to whom they gave the habit, according to the forms for investiture in the Ritual of Cîteaux.

Of their poverty more must be said. It was indeed extreme. They had in fact nothing to subsist on, but what they received of the charity of the Archbishop; but this was not all. As if to put their patience to the utmost trial, and make full experiment of their fidelity, Almighty God permitted that there should happen at that time a great famine, which desolated the whole country, reducing it to the last state of destitution. They had neither bread, money, nor any provision, and yet a great multitude of people, pressed by hunger, came upon them to beg for assistance. They sent to various persons in the neighbourhood to see if any help in these necessities might be in any way procured, but could obtain none. They knew not what to do. To quit the place, and abandon their undertaking, was a course which they refused to entertain for a moment; and yet how were they to remain in that solitude, having nothing to eat? That was impossible. They were soon brought to such distress, that for want of other food, they had to content themselves with wild roots and the leaves of the trees, mixed with salt and a little meal, to take away the bitterness of this unsavoury diet.

Such was the extremity to which they found themselves reduced—even their food, such as it was, was given by weight and measure; so scanty was the supply. How different in earthly blessings from the comfortable home of a Clugniac Abbey! Nevertheless, they none of them looked back to that "bread to the full," which they had then enjoyed; but blessed the Divine Providence, who still watched over them, for what He gave. They lived, in fact, not for themselves, but for the progeny which it should please God to give them. This hope stayed them amidst all their trials and difficulties. In the "sweat of their brow" they planted in the desert what was to be so fruitful a vine to the Lord. Against hope they believed in hope, that God might make their house a mother of Saints.

It may seem strange that the Monks should be reduced to such straits, when Thurstin had given to them the village of Sutton and its lands. It would appear that they surely from these sources would have enough for their subsistence. The reason why it was not so was, no doubt, that these poor villagers, being themselves in the greatest necessity, the good Monks did not press upon them for their dues.

An incident happened one day, which shows in a striking light to what an extent they carried forgetfulness of their own wants, to supply those of others. There knocked at the gate a poor man, demanding with urgency a piece of bread for the love of Jesus Christ. The Porter replied he had none. The poor man, however, became the more importunate on this refusal. He declared he was so famished with hunger, that he would not depart till he had received something. The Porter went to tell the Abbot, asking what was to be done. The Abbot, touched to the heart for the poor man, sent for the Brother who was over the larder, and ordered him to give some bread to the man. The Brother replied that there were only two loaves and a half left, and that these were for the carpenters to dine upon presently. "But," added he, "give one loaf, Reverend Father, to the poor man, and the rest to the workmen. As for us, the Lord knows how to provide, according to His will."

The Abbot approved of this advice, and ordered it to be executed. Well! at that very moment there arrived at the gate of the Monastery two men conducting a waggon loaded with bread of the most pure wheat flour. This had been sent to them as a supply for their need by Eustace Fitz-John, lord of Knaresborough Castle, who had learned, somehow, of their necessities. With what gratitude the Brethren received this present may be better conceived than narrated. They gave great thanks to God, and felt their confidence in His care reanimated by this very providential regard to their wants.

Nevertheless, God was not content with having proved their patience during this winter and the following summer; but as the sowing of their land was a difficult task during the first year, so their harvest was very bare and scanty; and for two years they had to endure the extreme of poverty. At last Richard, the Abbot, went to Clairvaux to represent the sad state of their affairs, and to beg the permission to emigrate into France. S. Bernard, touched with compassion, offered them one of the farms of his Monastery, at which they might reside till some more suitable place was found for them.

But God willed to preserve them for the edification of the English nation, and during the absence of Richard, the difficulties under which the Brethren laboured were removed. Hugh, Dean of York, a man of considerable wealth, joined the Community, endowing it with all his possessions, amongst which were copies of the Holy Scriptures. Thus commenced the library of the Abbey. They appropriated their new endowments to the use of the poor, the building of the Abbey, and the support of the Monks. Incited, probably, by this great example, Serlo, a Canon of York, rich both in gold and silver, and Foster, another Canon, gave themselves and their substance. These contributions were soon followed by a grant from Robert de Sartis, a military man living in the neighbourhood. He, with his wife Raganilda, gave the village of Harleshowe, with the lands adjacent, and the forest of Worksall. These benefactors were both buried at Fountains.

Other benefactors also were raised up by God, and soon the Abbey began to prosper, and the number of its Monks to increase. Clairvaux, founded by S. Bernard, had had to pass through a similar trial on its first formation. This Monastery was reduced to such a state of poverty, that the Monks were on the point of returning to Cîteaux, when God provided for their wants by raising up benefactors to assist them. By such a furnace it pleases Him to prove the fine gold; not that He is ignorant of its purity, but that others may see that there is no dross in it. "Ah," cries the author of their Annals, "how great was the perfection of those Monks! the fervour of their house! the exactitude of their discipline! Our Fathers and founders came from an Abbey rich and full of comforts. They became instead rich in virtues and filled with spiritual gifts. They were a spectacle of admiration to men and angels; and to their successors they transmitted the same perfection, as the most precious heritage and the greatest riches of which they could make them heirs."

Robert, from the moment he joined them, we are told, showed himself one already far advanced in the way of God. He was no idler, but knew well how to employ his hands in those penitential labours which form an integral part of the Cistercian life. He had a great zeal for them, and his ardour stirred up that of the rest. He was not, however, one of those who betray a zeal for work, because they have none for prayer. It may be said, indeed, that his mind was always with God; and that whilst his hands were actively busy with the occupations of earth, his soul was no less so with those of heaven. The one occupation did not hinder the other. If his counsels were asked on any matter, his words were simple and unaffected; but there was a depth of clear discernment in them, that showed them to be—not of earth, but of heaven—a ray of the living Light—a stream flowing from the Fountain of Eternal Wisdom and Truth. His counsel was not his own, but had for its source Him "in whom are hidden all the treasures of wisdom and knowledge."

CHAPTER V.

THE CISTERCIAN IDEA.

> "*La Religion, le front voilé, descend,*
> *Elle approche : déjà son calme attendrissant,*
> *Jusqu'au fond de votre âme en secret s'insinue ;*
> *Entendez-vous un Dieu dont la voix inconnue*
> *Vous dit tout bas : Mon fils, viens ici, viens à moi ;*
> *Marche au fond du désert : j'y serai près de toi.*"
> —CHATEAUBRIAND.

SOME little notice has been already taken of the difference between the old Benedictine and the Cistercian mode of life. At the first foundation of Cîteaux, great disputes had arisen between the reformed Benedictines, as the Cistercians professed themselves, and the Benedictines of the relaxed observance of the Rule. These disputes indeed became at times far too hot, and almost bitterly captious about trifles. Peter the Venerable says, that when a black Monk met any Cistercians, he would sometimes pretend to be frightened and scared at their white habit, and the Cistercians, on their part, would make some similar retaliation. There was a jealousy between the two Orders ; at least between those members of them, who were not thoroughly under the power of that divine charity, which "seeketh not her own, and is not easily provoked." Human weaknesses find their way into the cloister; and even Saints cannot be said to be altogether freed from their baneful influence. If, then, it is owned that too strong things were said and done on both sides, it is but owning that Monks are still men; and, though they make professed war against their evil passions, are not yet entirely exempt from those frailties which are the common lot of man.

The Cistercians and the old Benedictines were certainly awkwardly circumstanced for the exercise of mutual charity. They both maintained themselves to be guided by the same law, namely, the Rule of S. Benedict. Meanwhile, however, the Benedictines were favourers of the most lax interpretation of that law, and their practice fell even below their relaxed standard. The Cistercians, on the contrary, strained the minutiæ of the law to the utmost extent of rigour; and in their actual practice they far exceeded the austerities required by the law laid down.

S. Aelred, Abbot of Rievaux, in 1143, describing the life of his Monks, numbering about three hundred, says, "They drink nothing but water, eat little, and that coarse; labour hard, sleep little, and on hard boards; never speak, except to the Superior on necessary occasions; never refuse the burden they are ordered to carry; have not a moment for sloth or amusements of any kind; never have any law-suit or dispute." The Benedictines, on the contrary, not only drank wine, as allowed by the Rule, but of costly kinds; had plenty of food to eat, and of better quality than allowed by the Rule; used soft beds instead of the mattresses of straw ordered by S. Benedict; employed the hours of labour in study, copying books, painting, &c; easily broke the prescribed silence, and engaged in law-suits about their property. It may be seen from this that the rude life practised by Robert at Fountains, even when its extreme difficulties were over, was very different from his life at the Benedictine Abbey of Whitby.

It would be, however, impossible, without going deeply into the subject, to form a fair estimate of Robert's character as a Cistercian Saint.

When the band of Monks quitted S. Mary's of York, and when Robert obtained leave to join them, it was because a certain idea had taken fast hold of their minds, and this idea would not permit them to rest. It was their admiration of the Cistercian life. A burning avarice took possession of their breasts. A covetous thirst, not for gold or this world's wealth, comforts, or treasures, but for Cistercian poverty and want; for a share in those rude and hard labours undergone for Christ. How they longed to give up that life, which once they had thought so holy and so pure! Now it seemed to them a living death, a slothful and indolent profession, a bare and empty name, without the substance of the Monastic state. How they longed to get away out of the world, far away out of its sight—to break with it completely! The very being in its neighbourhood was misery. The noise of men, the sound of their busy traffic, had become hateful.

The quiet seclusion of a Cistercian Abbey, far away from the din of the city and the hum of men; this looked to their eyes like a heaven upon earth. The austere simplicity of the Cistercian Oratories—what a happy exchange for the pomp and fast of their own highly ornamented Churches. Awaking as it were from a deep sleep, they said with S. Augustine: "What aileth us? What are we about? we suffer the unlearned to rise up and take heaven by violence, whilst we, with all our knowledge, remain behind cowardly and without heart. What! because they have outstripped us are we ashamed to follow? Is it not more shameful still, not even to follow?"

Although a life of seclusion is not the ordinary vocation of man, yet there have in all ages of the world been institutions for exceptional cases. Monasticism had its precedents and models under the Old Testament. The schools of the Prophets, founded it is supposed by Samuel, were cenobitic institutions very similar to the Religious houses of Christianity. John the Baptist dwelt in the desert from his very childhood. So even, ancient heathenism had its vestal virgins. But what was shadowed forth in nature, and more distinctly expressed under the Mosaic Dispensation, was brought into full life by the Gospel. Christianity, preaching a contempt of all material goods, cut at the root of an earthly life by her doctrines of abnegation and mortification.

Various reasons have been given for the rise of Monasticism. The true one is, that by a life of seclusion and rigorous discipline so much assistance is afforded to the development of the more spiritual portion of man's being. The soul is so tied to its powers, that it is obliged to take part in all they do. If they flow forth in exterior works, it must of necessity diffuse itself, for they cannot act without it; and thereby its interior operations are considerably enfeebled. If the eye would see all, the ear hear all, the soul will be dispersed on all these objects. For this reason a certain doctor has said, "When man would work within, he must gather up all the powers of his soul into a corner, shut his eyes to all images and forms, forget and be ignorant of everything; then he can act." The occupations, therefore, of a life in the world, almost necessarily draw away and distract the soul from the contemplation of heavenly things. After the first days of the Christian dispensation, the Monastic life began to be practised. Paul of Thebes and S. Antony are called by S. Jerome the first hermits; but in 325, S. Pachomius erected the first Monastery. At the end of the fifth century Monasteries were to be found all over the Christian world. The fact of the movement being so rapid and general proves an antecedent disposition for this kind of life. The influence of Monastic Communities in spreading the Gospel, has been far greater than is ordinarily imagined. It was they who in a great measure prepared the way for the triumphs of Christianity. It is true that the solitaries in quitting the world, seemed to renounce the interests of their brethren; but on the other side, by the conquests of their passions, the austerity of their lives, the severe simplicity and holiness of their conversation, they became models, which both excited astonishment, and spurred on the masses of the faithful to endeavour at least in a measure, to free themselves from the slavery of the world and the flesh.

It has been stated in a former chapter, how S. Benedict and his sister S. Scholastica filled all Europe with their followers, and how in course of time, the Rule left by him began to be much relaxed. When, however, it is said that S. Odo of Clugni restored the practice of this Rule to its full vigour, it must be by no means understood that his Community practised the rigours of the first Cistercians. The Cistercian idea went far beyond the Rule laid down by S. Benedict. It was not content with its precepts, but followed out its counsels; its interpretations of the Rule being always on the side of austerity. The life of the primitive Cistercians may rather be called a reproduction of the severe rigours of the Egyptian

Monasteries, than that portrayed by the more mild Rule of the Western Patriarch.

Every Religious Order is said to have its peculiar spirit. The Sons of S. Francis are famed for holy poverty; those of S. Ignatius, for obedience; the Redemptorist has a childlike spirit; the Benedictine Monk is renowned for learning. The Religious life is the common possession of all: but the particular grace which distinguishes each Order is its own, and is not possessed by the others, in anything like the same degree of perfection. It is this which forms for it its peculiar distinctive character. Men are at once struck by it; for it gives its tone to every practice of the Order, diffusing itself everywhere, so that nothing escapes the penetrating influence of its spirit. With the Cistercians the animating principle of the Order was an austere, extreme simplicity. This may be called the "Cistercian Idea." This was the thing that astonished and appalled the world. To become a Cistercian Monk was to be bereft of everything that could please the senses, or flatter the pride of the intellect. This was truly leaving the world for the desert. It was like being entombed alive. Yet this very absence of all that could entice or allure, was the loadstone of attraction. This it was that drew to it S. Robert and his companions, and so many others, who desired to die to the world that they might live to God.

By examining more closely into the observance of the primitive Cistercians, it will be seen how this austere simplicity entered into, and was the animating principle of their new mode of life. First then, with regard to their food. By the rule of S. Benedict the use of the flesh of quadrupeds is forbidden to all, except those who are very weak or sickly. Many learned commentators infer from this, that he permits that of fowls; for why unnecessarily mention the word " quadruped" unless for the sake of distinction.

The discipline of Religious houses as that of the Church generally, both in East and West, has varied in different ages with respect to the kinds of food constituting abstinence. Socrates the historian says— "Some abstain from all animals, others eat fish only, others eat fowl with fish, believing them born from the waters, in consequence of the text, in which Moses records that the waters were commanded to produce them on the fifth day." This was a general interpretation from the fourth century, and seems to be authorised by S. Basil and S. Ambrose. In the most austere Religious Orders fowl and game were permitted at certain seasons. S. Columbanus fed his Monks with this food during a famine. Childeric invited S. Gregory of Tours to take some soup, adding that he might eat it as it was made of fowl. In Italy fowls are not esteemed a delicacy, and their flesh is not so gross or nourishing to the body as that of four-footed animals. The use of flesh meat, however, seems to be forbidden by chapter xxxix. All other articles of diet are freely allowed, such as eggs, fish, cheese, butter, milk, oil, &c. &c., provided that there be only two dishes of these; the third dish must be of fruit or uncooked vegetables.

The Cistercians went further. They contented themselves generally with two dishes of vegetables, cooked without grease or oil,—the third being only of fruit and salad, if it might be had. Butter, honey, eggs, milk, cheese, and fish were, it is true, allowable on all days out of Lent and Advent, with few exceptions; but they were not usually given unless on great Festival occasions. Vegetables and bread were the diet in Lent and Advent, fish being permissible to the exclusion of all else. Even the sick and the guests were subjected to this rule. The Monks fasted on bread and water on the last three Fridays of Lent. The bread was oftentimes only of barley or rye; and when of wheat, was never allowed to be of fine flour, but only of seconds, or coarser still. The use of pepper, and cumin, a herb then much prized, was forbidden; and the common garden herbs only allowed for seasoning.

S. Benedict allows a pint of wine each day for drink, though he concedes it rather unwillingly. The primitive Cistercians either used none at all, or only in smaller quantity. John the hermit, in his life of S. Bernard, tells us, that a Monk named Christian was planting a vine at Clairvaux, when Guy and Gerard, brothers of S. Bernard, passed by, and excommunicated the vine, telling him that wine was not the drink of Monks, and that he would never see the fruit of his vine. He died some time after; and the vine continuing unfruitful, S. Bernard was appealed to; he took off the curse by means of an aspersion of holy water, and thenceforward the vine began to bare fruit. S. Bernard permitted the use of wine, but drank next to none himself; and only advises a small quantity in case of necessity. There is so much nourishment in wine, even of the poorest sort, that no other drink could supply its place. Beer and other made drinks were sometimes used by the Cistercians, where they did not take wine, but often water only served their purpose. Such was the austere simplicity of the articles of their table. From the fourteenth of September till Easter, they ate but once a day. This single meal, out of Lent was at about half-past two o'clock; in Lent, after four. During the other half of the year, the principal repast took place at half-past eleven; and a lesser one at six o'clock, at which they had no dressed dish, but only fruit, salad, &c., with a small quantity of bread.

With regard to their clothing, it was of course frieze undyed, the colour being gray rather than white, as may be seen from a Cowl of S. Bernard's, still preserved in the Church of S. Victor at Paris. The change from black to this colour was introduced by S. Alberic, on the ground of cheapness and simplicity, dye being then an expensive article. They were allowed no underclothing. A robe, with sleeves strait at the wrist, covered the body; over this was a Cowl and a hood, the Cowl being a more ample robe reaching to the feet, with loose sleeves. A girdle, shoes and stockings, complete the whole dress. It is related of S. Bernard, that when his health was in so deplorable a state as to demand every relief, he would not consent to wear a woollen shirt in addition to the above articles of dress, till obliged by an order of the Sovereign Pontiff. For work, a scapular supplied the place of the Cowl, covering the head and the shoulders. If cold, they were allowed to wear two robes or Cowls. They kept a strict silence perpetually, day and night, unless when obliged to speak to Superiors on necessary matters.

S. Benedict's Rule gives a little more then six hours for work daily throughout the year. The Choir-Monks, for the most part, employed this time in the farm or garden. Some, it is true, copied books in the Scriptorium, but not the major part of the Community. S. Benedict supposes, that in case of extreme poverty, Monks might have to gather in themselves the produce of their land; but with the Cistercians this was an indispensable feature of their life. The great S. Bernard boasts of his powers as a good reaper. During the harvest there was generally extra work; and they sometimes took their meridian sleep in the open air.

But it was in their Churches that their characteristic simplicity appeared in the most striking manner. Many other Saints have desired to see an evangelical poverty, even in the furniture of the Sanctuary; but none ever came up to the first Cistercians in this matter. Their manner of worship afforded a most astonishing contrast to the habitual pomp of the Cathedral, Collegiate and Benedictine Churches, nay, even of many parish Churches. In their singing, which was slow and solemn, no harmonised parts were introduced, but all the voices sang in unison.

The ornaments of the Church, and of the Ministers of the altar, were of the most simple description. Ornamented pavement, mosaic work, or tiles of different colours were strictly proscribed. In 1235, when the Abbot of Gard had violated this rule, he was condemned to break up his pavement. The ancient usages of Citeaux forbade all stained glass in their Churches. In 1182 the General Chapter ordered the demolition of all stained windows set up contrary to this prescription; giving only the delay of two years for the fulfilment of its definition.

The Institutes of the General Chapter prohibit every species of sculpture as useless. The General Chapter of 1213 permits nothing else to be painted, except the image of the Saviour. Cæsarius in his dialogues tells us of a Benedictine Monk, who died at the commencement of the thirteenth century, and who was very much esteemed for the excellence of his productions. This Monk painted over the Altars of many Cistercians Abbeys, crucifixes of a truly admirable beauty. He would take no salary, but only the actual expenses of his work. This Monk died on a Good Friday. In 1240 the General Chapter having learned that some Altars of Cistercian Churches were beautified, ordered all the ornamentation to be done away with; allowing only that the altar might be painted white. Spite of this prohibition, the Abbot of Royeaumont had the audacity to cause an altar to be adorned with paintings, sculpture, curtains, and columns, surmounted with Angels. He was ordered to destroy all within a month, under pain of being deprived together with his Prior of his allowance of wine, until the definition should be executed. It is not difficult, therefore, to comprehend what is related of the visit of Pope Innocent II. to Clairvaux in 1131, when it is said, he could see in the Church nothing but the four bare walls.

At the commencement of the Abbotship of Stephen Harding, the Cistercians held a council, in which it was determined to receive no more sacred vessels or ornaments, not only as contrary to that poverty, of which they make so particular a profession, but as likely to give birth to desires of having other different things, which might content and flatter the curiosity of the mind, rather than serve to edify piety.

To cut off all superfluity and magnificence, they sent away the gold and silver cross, determining for the future to be content with one of painted wood. They would only retain one candlestick,* and that of iron. It was decreed that Copes, Dalmatics, and Tunicles must never be used in Cistercian Churches; that the Chasubles must be each of a single colour, and without orphreys. They as well as the stoles and maniples must be made of some common material, not of silk, and must have no ornament or fringe of gold or silver. The palls and all the other altar linen were to be perfectly plain. No cruets either of gold or silver must be used. The Censer was ordered to be of brass or iron. In the eighteenth century there was still shown a chasuble of cotton, worn by S. Bernard. Such was the simplicity of these first Cistercians. It gave great scandal to the Clugniacs who taxed them with extreme rigour. S. Bernard defends this simplicity, whilst he inveighs against the magnificence of Benedictine Churches. "I speak not," he says to William, a Clugniac Abbot, "of the immense height, length, and width of their Churches, of the sumptuous embellishments and curious paintings one sees on every side; which, attracting the eyes of the worshippers, turn their minds from prayer; and in some sort represent to me the ancient Jewish rite :—but let that pass—Let all these things be done for the glory of God. This question, however, I ask,

---

* This candlestick stood not on the Altar, but on the pavement near to the Altar. It was generally highly ornamented and made of brass, silver, or even gold.

as a Monk of Monks—a question with which a heathen chid his heathen brethren. '*Dicite*,' says he, '*Pontifices, in sancto quid facit aurum.*' And I say, tell me, ye poor, if poor ye are, (for I regard the sense rather than the words,) tell me, what is gold doing in your Churches? and here let me say, that Monks must not plead as Bishops. We know that they are debtors to the wise and to the unwise. Not being able to stir up the devotion of a carnal people by spiritual exercises, they excite it by these exterior ornaments. But as for us who have come out of the people,—who, for the sake of Jesus Christ, have quitted all that the world counts precious and beautiful,—who have rejected as dung and ordure all that flatters the senses,—whether what is pleasing to the sight, soothing to the ear, sweet to the smell, delightful to the taste, or agreeable to the touch; by the use of these things whose devotion is it we would excite? what fruit is it we expect from these things, unless the admiration of fools, and the offerings of the simple? Is it not, that having mingled amongst the nations, ye have learned their works, and serve their idols?

"To speak plainly, is not avarice, which is a service of idols, at the bottom of all this? It is not fruit we look for, but gifts. If you ask, How? by a wonderful manner I answer. Since by the sight of this display, magnificence, and delectable vanities, men are excited to offer rather than to pray. Thus wealth drinks in wealth, and money, more money. The more riches are beheld, (strange reason, why it is so I know not,) the more is therefore offered.* Coronas, or rather huge wheels, glittering more with precious stones than with the lamps they sustain, are hung in their Churches; and, instead of candlesticks, trees of brass marvellously wrought by the artificer, casting forth more light from their jewels, than from the candles placed upon them.—And what is the object of these things? Is it the compunction of penitents that is sought for, or the admiration of the spectators? vanity of vanities, yea, rather insane folly than vanity. The Church is splendid in her edifices, and in her poor is in penury. Her stones are clothed with gold, and her children are left naked. The eyes of the rich are pandered to at the expense of the needy. The curious are delighted, but the miserable find no sustenance. And what accord is there between these superfluities, and those who have made a vow of poverty, religious spiritual men?"

* This is an allusion to a Corona of lights given to Clugni by Matilda Queen of England, made after the pattern mentioned in Exodus xxv. It was made of gold and silver, and its delicate branches blazed with crystals and beryls, interspersed amidst beautifully-wrought lilies.

CHAPTER VI.

INFLUENCE OF FOUNTAINS—FOUNDATION OF NEWMINSTER.

" *Le fantôme du siècle, emporté par le temps,*
Passe, et roule autour d'eux ses pompes mensongères;
Mais c'est en vain : du siècle ils ont fui les chimères ;
Hormis l'éternité, tout est songe pour eux.
Pénétrez avec moi ces murs religieux :
N'y respirez-vous pas l'air paisible des cieux ?
Vos chagrins ne sont plus, vos passions se taisent ;
Et du cloître muet les ténèbres vous plaisent."
—CHATEAUBRIAND.

THE holy Community of Fountains Abbey were most strict and fervent in their observation of the Cistercian mode of life. Geoffrey seems unable to contain his admiration at the humility, and docile obedience, with which they followed out the instructions he was sent to give them.

In the year 1127, there came as a visitor to the Abbey a noble gentleman, Ralph de Merlay. He had already heard something of the kind of life led by the Monks of the Cistercian Order. Being a man of great piety, he desired with his own eyes to bear witness to what he had heard of them. It cannot be surprising that he was greatly moved at the sight of their blameless conversation and austere penance. S. Bernard declares that when he first entered Religion, the very sight of some of the Monks, nay, even the remembrance of them when absent or dead, so deeply impressed him with tender sentiments of the love of God, that oftentimes tears would fall from his eyes in abundance. S. Paul says of true Christians, "We are the good odour of Jesus Christ." Such were these Monks of Fountains. Men felt that it was good to be in their company, because their very presence breathed forth an atmosphere of sanctity. Their emaciated countenances, lit up by the brightness of an ineffable interior gladness, were a sermon more powerful than the most eloquent words could utter. Indeed, if the pictures and images of the Saints affect us with such feelings of devotion, with how much more force must their living presence appeal to the feelings of the heart? Pope Innocent II., we are told, when visiting Clairvaux, could not satiate his eyes sufficiently with gazing on the ravishing beauty of holiness, which so sweetly beamed forth from the faces of the Monks.

Ralph de Merlay filled with holy compunction, the Lord so inspiring him for the redemption of his soul, offered the Abbot a plot of ground on his own estate in Northumberland, begging that a Colony of Monks from Fountains might be granted him, that thus he might always have near him some of these servants of God.

The Community of Fountains was now large and well instructed, it being five years from the first foundation of the Abbey. The Abbot therefore willingly received the offer made him by this good gentleman.

The admiration with which Ralph de Merlay was filled at the Cistercian mode of life, and his great desire to found a like Monastery on his own property, may seem to some an astonishing thing. We live in a dark age, when the obscured vision of most men can only behold the advantages of those schemes, which further some earthly object, such as the advancement of arts or secular learning. It comes to pass, therefore, that even by good men the Monastic way of life is secretly undervalued. It is looked upon as a quaint and obsolete thing, a thing of the middle ages, which might with no great disadvantage be quietly suffered to die out. Monks may be very good and holy persons, but of what use are they? Any Religious Order which takes charge of Schools, Refuges, Orphanages, Hospitals, &c., is appreciated, because social progress seems assisted by such Institutions.

But if any one, having enough of talent and ability to be actively useful in the world, enter a Contemplative Order, it is esteemed so much waste of what might have been otherwise profitable. This is the view of modern times, but it was not that of the ages of faith. It is the view taken by shallow minds, but not that of deep thinkers. It is the view of those who have a smattering of piety, but not that of the Saints. Lastly, it is the view of human prudence, but is not that of Eternal Wisdom or of the Church.

The life of the Church is a sort of continuation and extension of the life of Jesus Christ, in and through His members. What He began in His own person He continues in them by a living tradition. But there are certain phases of the life of Jesus, which could never receive their legitimate expression in His Church, except in the contemplative life. Thus the picture of His hidden life at Nazareth is especially portrayed and developed by Orders such as the Cistercian. The active and mixed life corresponds more with the three years of His ministry. Again, if we had only the life of the routine Christian to go to, the higher portions of the teaching of Christ would be mere empty sounds, like the doctrines of the ancient pagan philosophers, who indeed spoke well, but gave no power to put into practice the teaching they put forward. If the truth must be spoken, the greater number of Christians consider the doctrines of the Divine Master to be admirable indeed in theory; but that to make them the guide of their conduct would be a great piece of foolishness.

The doctrine of Jesus Christ calls poverty blessed; but who does not know that the generality of Christians shun poverty as a pest? Jesus Christ exhorts to choose the lowest place; but who considers that he ought to practise this rule? Jesus Christ tells us to take up the cross, and count ourselves blessed if we suffer and are persecuted; but who is there that does not shrink from all that affects his ease and comfort? He tells us to study as an example the littleness and simplicity of a child; but each one on the contrary wishes to be esteemed wise, prudent, and clever. Thus the world, even the world of professing Christians, may be said to hold in abhorrence the maxims of Jesus Christ. He must go elsewhere if he wishes to obtain disciples of doctrines so extravagant and lofty.

This being the case, God is pleased to draw away from the multitude of the people certain chosen souls, who shall bear testimony by their life, both to the practicability of the doctrines of His Son, and to the great happiness obtained by following out His counsels. These souls become living exemplars of His teaching. They are an impersonification of His doctrine, to whom He can point and appeal, as to a living epistle, speaking loudly against all the world's maxims, ways of acting and thinking. Christ indemnifies Himself by their fidelity and fervour for the coldness, contempt, and neglect, with which He finds Himself and His doctrines treated by the mass of professing Christians.

The disciple is bound to uphold the doctrine of his preceptor, and the doctrine of Christ is no mere philosophy of words. It cannot be upheld as a mere speculative science. It must be written on the body and soul—written in actions and sufferings. The doctrine of Christ is so difficult of comprehension, that no other arguments than these will be considered to have any weight, or produce any amount of conviction. Men must be seen flying the vain pomp of the world, seeking obscurity, contempt, abjection, poverty, and want. They must be seen giving up their own will, their own ways and desires; living in voluntary subjection; voluntarily undergoing privation; withdrawing from honours; not only resigned under, but seeking crosses. They must be seen employed in the lowest and meanest occupations, toiling for their daily bread, and eating it in the sweat of their brow. Such disciples may be called guarantees for the truth of the doctrines of Christ. Without their living testimony, the higher maxims of His teaching would be unproved, unwitnessed to. The Cistercian Monasteries were schools of Christ, in which most perfect discipline abounded. The immense majority of the Monks were men of the highest ranks of society. These being rich, for Christ's sake, became poor. They lived like the very serfs by the labour of their hands. S. Bernard, speaking of miracles, says that the greatest he ever witnessed, was to behold day after day men, who might be great and honoured in the world, living in an open prison, voluntarily subjecting themselves to labours, contempt, poverty, and all sorts of privations.

It is the interest of the world to throw scandal on Religion by representing it as an eccentric melancholy. The world well knows that if the truth came out, it would find many of its admirers leaving its ranks, and deserting over to the cause of Christ. It is for this purpose, that to keep up the illusion, it sets off its own vain and tasteless joys by the slander and detraction of those of God. For the graces of God, given to those who advance courageously in the ways of piety, are like an excellent meat. And those who have tasted this most agreeable food, find in it such abundance of sweetness, that it makes them despise all else. They would not for the world use any mixture of other diet, lest it should impair, in any measure, the savour of that which is so exceedingly delicious. The marvellous contentment they feel surpasses all that can be conceived, so that there is no reason to wonder at their having a disgust of all the pleasures of this life. They can afford to despise the things of earth who have tasted " of the heavenly gift, and of the powers of the world to come," and have been given to drink of the fulness of that " torrent which maketh glad the city of God."

The Community of Fountains Abbey having embraced the austere poverty of Christ, had been endowed also richly with those qualities of a heavenly mind, which made them appear to be rather angels than men. The beauty and exquisite perfume of the lily has an additional charm, because it is found growing amongst the thorns. So the humble occupations of these Cistercians, and their austere lives, lent an additional attraction to the sweetness of their character. There was a certain indescribable gracefulness in their every word and action, which ravished the heart of Ralph de Merlay, a gracefulness not consisting in worldly polish, but in a something supernatural, which overflowed from the presence of Christ within them. And this tinged and gave a holy charm to the meanest things, so that things, the most trivial in themselves, appeared somehow in a different light when done by them; why or how, it was difficult to say, but easy to feel. A sort of mystic unction seemed to pour itself around them, steeping and penetrating with its fragrant balm everything they touched.

It has ever been so, and will ever be so with saintly persons. A virtue goes forth from them without their will or knowledge, and those who are brought within its sphere, cannot subtract themselves from its influence, though they may resist it. Ralph de Merlay was not of those who resist. His heart was won. He would have some of these servants of God near him, and "be at charges" for them; in order that some of those favourable glances, directed by God towards them, might fall to his lot.

Wherever the true disciples of the cross are seen,

there will be also found the homage paid to them by the rich and noble. It began at Bethlehem in the person of their Master, when the Wise men came from the East to pour their treasures at the foot of the manger-cradle. It showed itself at Calvary in the burial given to the Crucified by the wealthy Joseph of Arimathea. It is but the fulfilment of the promise made by God in the mystical language of the prophet: "The labour of Egypt, and the merchandise of Ethiopia and Saba, men of stature shall come over to thee, and be thine. They shall walk after thee; they shall go bound with manacles, and shall worship thee, and shall make supplication unto thee. Only in thee is God. They shall worship thee with their face towards the earth, and shall lick up the dust of thy feet."

Ralph de Merlay having obtained a promise of a Colony, returned in joy and gladness to Morpeth, to prepare for their reception. The Brethren remained at Fountains over the fifth anniversary of the foundation of the Abbey, and then Robert, with twelve others, started for Northumberland. They arrived after three days' journey, and were received by Ralph de Merlay in his castle, on the first day of January 1138. The spot destined for their future habitation was an ample domain, a beautiful place with water, and having a fair wood about it. They at once took possession, and as there is no account of any hardships through which they had to pass, it may be supposed that there were already some farm buildings on the spot, sufficient to provide for their wants, till the Abbey should be more conveniently constructed.* It must also be borne in mind that those lordly buildings, which are so justly admired for the beauty of their architecture, were not built in the first age of the Cistercian Order, but were the production of a later period of its annals.

The first Monasteries of the Cistercians were of a very humble character, suited to that simplicity and austere poverty, of which they made so special a profession. The first Church at Cîteaux, in which S. Stephen and S. Alberic were buried, was but fifteen feet wide, having only three windows in the sanctuary and two in the nave.

About the Day of the Epiphany, Robert being freely and canonically elected by his Brethren, Geoffrey, Bishop of Durham came over and consecrated him Abbot.

There can be no greater proof of the very high esteem Robert had attained in the space of five years, by his manner of life amongst the Community of Fountains, than that he should be chosen Abbot of the new Monastery. It was not in the ordinary course of things, that one, who was comparatively a stranger, should be fixed upon to occupy the important and

* The first Monastery was destroyed a year after its construction by King David of Scotland, who behaved very cruelly to the Monks.

responsible post of commencing a new foundation; especially when there can be no doubt that amongst the emigrants from S. Mary's Abbey, there were those who would have been perfectly qualified for the task. The virtues of Robert's character must have been in a remarkable degree supereminent, to account for his being so chosen in preference to any one else. He had for the sake of God given up his position, the respect, love, and esteem, in which he was held, to go and become the last and lowest of the Community of Fountains. God now raised him up to the place of ruler of the new Monastery.

CHAPTER VII.

ROBERT'S LOVE OF SOULS—LIFE OF THE CLOISTER.

> "*With the love of a mother*
> *His chosen to tend,*
> *With the zeal of a brother, to keep and defend.*
> *In vigil unwearied,*
> *In fasting and prayer,*
> *Lest harm should befall those left in thy care."*
> —SONGS OF CHRISTIAN CHIVALRY.

ROBERT, therefore, was made Abbot, and it was wonderful to behold how those graces and virtues, with which his soul was already so richly endowed, seemed suddenly to spring forth into a new and more abundant life. It was as if hitherto they had been kept under restraint, pent up within too narrow bounds, and could only now abandon themselves with free scope to the full exercise of all the energy of their character. This was due no doubt in a measure to those exertions, which all men of high spirit make, to acquit themselves worthily of any responsible charge; but it was partly also the effect of the particular graces of the Abbatial Benediction.

The grace of God was not given to him in vain, but he laboured earnestly to fulfil the work of the Ministry intrusted to him. He knew what S. Benedict says of the Abbot, namely, that he will have to give an account not only of his own soul, but of the souls of all who have been intrusted to his charge; and that if the Master of the house discover that he has suffered any diminution of profit in his sheep, the blame will fall on the Abbot. Only then shall he be esteemed clear in the judgment of God, when he has in vain used all diligence towards a disobedient flock.

Bearing therefore in mind, that the care of their eternal salvation was committed to him, and considering how great the guilt must be if, through any neglect on his part, any of those sheep should perish for whom Christ died, Robert watched over the souls of his Brethren as one that must give account, that he might do it with joy and not with grief. He was a true Abbot. He had a father's heart. There are some Superiors who content themselves with admonishing their subjects of their duty. There they leave the matter. They have relieved their conscience. But what comfort is it to a father's heart, that he has admonished a froward son, when he sees that son being led to the gallows? Robert loved his Brethren. The thought of seeing any of them weeping and howling in the burning lake, filled him with dismay. He never could feel satisfied, unless he saw by their conduct that they were such as Christ would have them be; such as might pass at the bar of God—real and true Monks. It was for this he wept, and sighed, and made prayers night and day before God, filling his mouth with arguments in their favour. For this he reproved, entreated, and rebuked; was instant in season and out of season. For this he braved their displeasure, whilst he courted their love. For this he walked before them blameless, that nothing might be wanting to allure and incite them to pursue the good way, leading to life eternal. He wished to be able one day to present them to the Lord holy and without blemish, without spot or wrinkle or any such thing; so that he might see them shining like stars of the firmament in the kingdom of their Father.

But once as he was making his prayers with more earnestness than usual, and, with tears of compunction trickling down his cheeks, was pouring forth his soul before God, beseeching that as well his own, as the service of his Brethren, might be acceptable to the Divine Majesty, and that they might be found worthy to have their names written in the book of life, there came a voice from heaven, speaking after this manner: "Be of good comfort, my son, for thy prayers have been heard; and the names of the sons for whom thou hast besought Me are written in heaven. Only two of them, whose hearts were fixed on the love of earthly things, are written in the earth." Not long after, two of the lay brethren, having cast off the habit of Religion, made a miserable end of their lives in the world; and thus the holy man saw the verification of the revelation he had received.

And here, perhaps, is the fitting place to relate another event which occurred on a certain occasion during the singing of the divine office, by which may be seen also with what solicitude Robert watched over his Brethren, and how great was the effect of his holy prayers in their behalf. One night, whilst the Monks were at Vigils, he saw the malignant Enemy standing at the door of the Choir, oftentimes endeavouring to enter, but in vain. He appeared under the guise of a country fellow, with long and naked limbs, carrying at his back a basket, and having a bundle of wood tied before his breast with cords. With outstretched neck he began to cast his eyes around the Choir, attentively considering the Brethren, to see if he could not discover something favourable to his bad purpose in some one of them. But as the man of God applied himself earnestly in prayer to God, stirring up the hearts of his Brethren to devotion, the infernal spy perceiving that, after his long expectation, he yet gained no advantage, with great anger turned away and betook himself to the Choir of the laybrethren. There gazing curiously at each, if he saw any one sleeping he chuckled scornfully; if he found any occupied with dishonest thoughts, he exulted with marvellous satisfaction. At length, among the novices, he found a youth letting his mind wander forth to illicit desires, only present in body, and even then meditating a secret flight from the house. Seeing that this poor Brother was just fit for his purpose, he caught hold of him with a hook, and stowing him away in his basket, made all haste to be gone with his booty.

The holy man having seen this vision, thought that it boded no good, and was moved with great anxiety for the salvation of this man. As soon as it was morning, he sent a Brother to look for him, but, after a diligent search, the unfortunate youth was nowhere to be found. Alas, he had shaken off the sweet yoke of Christ: and before the dawn of day was gone forth as a wanderer and a vagabond, following the voice of the Enemy. Having left the Monastery he joined a band of wicked men, and became a robber. Not long had he been engaged in these evil courses, when being captured he was beheaded, and so came to a miserable end. We live in a Sadducean age, which cannot bring itself to believe in what are styled the mediæval legends, a judicious biographer of S. Robert might therefore perhaps be inclined to soften down those parts of his history, which jar with the feelings and ideas of the age. But what good would come of it? If the lives of Saints must be adapted to suit the prejudiced opinions of the men of any age, then there is an end to Christianity. Christianity deals in the marvellous from its very outset. It is an essential part of its character. Do away with the marvellous, and it becomes a maimed thing.

It is easy to reject as dreams, or pious fables, all

the wonderful things that are related in the lives of the Saints. But such a method of dealing with them is neither honest nor satisfactory. Nature's dominion is enlarged to an utterly incredible extent, to make out a solution for a multitude of facts and phenomena, formerly attributed to the agency of good or evil spirits, and yet of these phenomena nature is no sufficient cause. Men do violence to common sense and reason, to prevent being obliged to confess that there is in operation at their elbow an invisible spiritual world.

And although man is not pure spirit like the angels, yet being spirit as well as body, there is no reason for disbelieving that he can be brought into relation with the world of spirits. It is indeed exceedingly wrong for any one *directly* to thrust himself forward into these untraversed regions, yet there can be no doubt that the practice of the ascetical life *indirectly* tends to that end. In the ordinary state man differs little from the rest of the animal creation in the entertainment of his material life; but it is quite otherwise with those whom God calls to a mystical union with Himself, and to a participation of the miraculous powers of the God-man.

The entry into the mystical way cannot be made but by declaring a war of extermination against all natural appetites. This is an indispensable pre-requisite. Man must resign himself to undergo an entire modification of his being—a modification which cannot be produced without anguish. What is life to the soul is death to the body. If the soul therefore mounts to the loftier paths of the mystical life, it must be at the expense of the body. The body throws hindrances in the way, and these hindrances cannot be removed without pain. When a man has made some advance along the mystical pathway, the soul in a measure breaks off the yoke of the body, and reasserts that lordship which belonged to it in Adam, before sin had destroyed the harmony, which, at man's original creation, existed between the body and the soul. The superior element of man again resumes the preponderance, and that commerce between him and the invisible world, which was interrupted by sin, is recommenced. Man enters again in a measure on the privileges of his primitive state. The world of spirits, with its deep firmament of stars and its dark abysses, is laid open to him. The eye, the ear, and all the other senses, touch, taste, and smell, are exercised after a certain analogy to the bodily functions, by the soul, in a supernatural and spiritual manner.

God accords these graces when, how, and to whom, He pleases; but severe ascetical training is ordinarily the road which must first be traversed. This training breaks down that wall of flesh, whose grossness hinders the soul from the free exercise of her faculties. By seclusion and retirement it hinders her from dissipating their force through the distracting claims of a thousand conflicting objects. An interior training accompanies and marches alongside of the exterior. This consists in the renouncement and subjection of a man's own will, and the attachment he naturally has to the lights of his own intellect. The result of this bruising of nature is a continual ascension of the superior over the inferior part of the soul, and a greater clearness in the interior, which, by the help of the divine light, gives to the soul the sight of what was formerly enveloped in obscurity. It is not therefore to be thought strange if, without at all having sought it, she sometimes find herself as it were in actual contact with the powers of the unseen world. The veil has been partially drawn aside—the wall has been broken, and she sees through the chinks in it.

S. Robert is an instance in point; and it is in the histories of the Cistercian Saints, and of the Fathers of the Desert, that we find, in the greatest profusion, records of the marvellous and supernatural. It is precisely on account of their severe asceticism, which predisposed them for the operations of God. Let it, however, be stated that no one is obliged to believe the particular miracles related of S. Robert, or any other Saint, even though they be found in the Roman Breviary, as matters of faith. We may reject, or accept, as we please, according as their authentication appears to us sufficient or insufficient. They stand or fall on the ordinary ground of human testimony as given to other historical facts. But to disbelieve in the miraculous altogether is not so much to be termed incredulity, as sheer obstinacy and folly. But as our Lord is at one time to be seen working as a humble artizan in the carpenter's shop, at another time stilling the storm, or raising the dead, so the lives of His Saints are a strange mixture of the ordinary and extraordinary. The common round and daily task are the steps in the ladder, by which ascent to union with God is begun, continued, and ended. Thus are the heights of contemplation attained.

The life of the Cloister is not, as some have imagined, an inactive ecstasy of prayer, but is a judicious union of prayer and labour, modelled on that of the Holy Family. The examples of Our Lord, the Holy Virgin, and S. Joseph, suffice to show that the most exalted sanctity is to be found hedged in by quiet and humble labour. A well-ordered Monastery is a little beehive, where each one without noise or tumult is labouring diligently to fulfil his work in quiet and silence, so that there is to be seen in it a business-like tone, that would not disgrace a mercantile or industrial establishment. It comes to pass, therefore, that when a postulant presents himself, whose piety consists in a dislike of labour on pretence of a love of prayer and reading, he finds that a Monastery is far from being the refuge he took it for, and that he will have to work as much or more than when in the world; he therefore soon finds a pretext for retiring from such a kind of life. S. Robert was admirably suited for Abbot, because he was himself, as it were, a living exemplar of the virtues of the Monastic state. And as the sight of their General mixing in the thick of the fight spurs on the most cowardly to deeds of valour, so does the example of the Abbot, partaking in those humiliating and painful exercises, for which corrupt nature has such a repugnance, rouse to their duty even the most hard and unteachable. It may be conceived, then, what a treasure he was to his Monks. He was not like the Abbot Cæsarius speaks of, as having appeared to one of his Monks after death, the upper part of his body beautiful, but his lower parts disfigured. This Abbot was suffering much because, though diligent at prayer, he absented himself without occasion from labour. Robert, where he could, took part in the commonest and meanest labours, according to the counsel of the wise man, "Have they made thee ruler, be not lifted up, but be among them as one of them." As the violet, however, betrays her hiding-place by the sweetness of her perfume, so it was impossible for this man of God to conceal his sanctity by the meanness of his exterior employments. Excellence of a high order requires no extrinsic helps, it is sufficient for itself; the Majesty of the Incarnate God never appears greater than when lying a helpless Babe on a little straw. This sublime anomaly imprints itself on the heart, and causes sentiments of adoring homage to flow forth, that no amount of exterior splendour would have called up. So it was, that the humility of the employments of S. Robert served to make his sanctity the more admirable.

One day, when the holy man had been visiting one of the granges of the Abbey, which was at some distance; as a great festival was approaching, he wished to get back to Newminster. He had no palfrey, so he ordered to be made ready for him a pack-horse, whose employment was generally to be loaded with the bread for the granges. Having mounted this sorry nag, he pulled his hood half over his face, and began to pray and meditate as was his wont. As he was thus quietly making his way along, he was aroused from his meditation by a voice, which asked him, without ceremony and rather roughly, if he had seen the Lord Abbot in the place he was coming from. It was a nobleman who had come on business to the Abbey, and being told that the Abbot was at this grange, he was come to seek him. He had never the thought that this shabby figure on the pack-horse could be the object of his search, but supposed that it was one of the lay-brethren. Robert did not choose to undeceive him, so he said shrewdly, " When I was last at the grange the Abbot was there." There was something about the way and tone this equivocal answer was delivered, which made the nobleman look more closely at the speaker's features; and when he saw Robert's saintly face, he felt sure that, unawares, he was speaking with the Abbot. Having assured himself that he had the Abbot before him, he now strove to make amends for his first uncourteous salutation; and feeling ashamed to be on his fine horse, whilst the man of God was mounted on such a sorry beast, he got down; and nothing could satisfy him but that the Abbot must mount in his place, and so they returned to Newminster; where, having completed the business on which he had come, he humbly knelt for his blessing, and so departed.

The granges of the Cistercian Order were solely occupied by lay brothers, unlike the Cells of the Benedictines, who charged the Choir Monks with the care of their rural property. They were in arrangement not unlike Abbeys, having a dormitory, refectory, and Oratory. Mass, however, was never said in them. The Brothers had to go for Mass to the Abbey, at least on Sundays and those twenty-three Festivals on which no work was done.

Monks were obliged by the Cistercian Rule to know the whole of David's Psalter by heart, a thing necessary for the Choir Service at a time when books were scarce. Sometimes an Abbey of six hundred Monks had no more than five or six Psalters. S. Robert, besides the psalms sung in Choir, used to recite the whole Psalter every day. This he did doubtless during the time of labour, or other occupations, to keep his mind fixed on God. He also composed a beautiful Commentary on the Psalms for his Monks, which was greatly valued, but which has not been preserved to our days. Severe fasting was added to his prayer. His appetite he never fully satisfied. During Lent he permitted nothing to it but bread and water, and that in small quantity; but we must not suppose this mortification was done without inconvenience, or that the flesh made no rebellion against the penitence imposed on it. That region of the soul which is charged with administering the lower functions of life, may be to a certain point purified, disengaged, and elevated by the mortification of the flesh; but penitences the most rude can never altogether stifle its voice. It knows how from time to time to demand, with more or less imperiousness, its natural rights. A reaction succeeds that exhaustion to which it has been reduced. Then it is that it makes to be felt its solicitations for some relief. So it came to pass, that once at the time of Easter, Robert had so utterly mortified his stomach, and overthrown all appetite and gust for food, that it began to retaliate by refusing to take any of the accustomed diet.

The Brother who waited on him, said, "Father, why do you not eat?" "Ah!" said Robert, "if I could have a little oat cake moistened with butter, I think I should be able to eat of it with pleasure." But when the Brother had made it ready for him, the man of God, reflecting within himself that he was giving some indulgence to the lust of the appetite, was struck with horror at the sensuality he had been betrayed into; and determined to revenge himself on his body, for what he esteemed the unruliness of its desires. He, therefore, refused absolutely even to taste of what he had asked for; and, as David poured out on the ground, before the Lord, the water he had so longed for, so this servant of God remained altogether fasting; and commanded that the food he had coveted with over-eagerness, should be given to the poor, who waited at the Monastery gate. When the Monk went with the dish to the gate, he found there a fair young man of a very beautiful countenance, who, taking the dish into his hands with what was upon it, presently vanished. This wonderful thing they went and told to the Abbot; when lo! as they were all in wonder relating the marvel, the dish descended from above upon the table before the man of God. Whereby it was seen that he who had received the alms, was either an Angel, or the Lord of Angels Himself.

CHAPTER VIII.

THE PHILOSOPHY OF ASCETICISM.

> *"The women of old Rome were satisfied*
> *With water for their beverage; Daniel fed*
> *On pulse, and wisdom gained. The primal age*
> *Was beautiful as gold, and hunger then*
> *Made acorns tasteful,—thirst each rivulet*
> *Run nectar. Honey and locusts were the food*
> *Whereof the Baptist in the wilderness*
> *Fed, and that eminence of glory reached—*
> *That greatness which the Evangelist records."*
> —DANTE.

THERE is something in the practice of great austerities which, at first sight, appears in the eyes of men very unnatural, nay, even wrong, and highly censurable. We cannot comprehend the use or the lawfulness of treating the body with so great harshness. It appears to us a sort of fanaticism; and our impulse is at once loudly to condemn it. If we suspend our judgment, it is because faith has taught us this lesson; but it is only when instructed by a special light of the Holy Ghost that we can appreciate what is so repugnant to the natural mind.

There certainly is a difficulty in the matter, and the natural mind seems to have good and sound reasons for the view it takes. For can it be supposed, it may be asked, that such cruelty to the body is agreeable to God? When God has provided for man things not only for his absolute necessities, but for his comfort, is it not His intention that man should with thanksgiving, temperately enjoy these good gifts? Is not the rejection of them an injury to the goodness of God, an affront to His kind Providence? Is not this to represent God after the manner of the heathen; as one who takes pleasure in the spectacle of frightful tortures, inflicted on the human frame in His honour. Thus it is that reason speaks, when yet untaught by faith, and unenlightened by the Holy Ghost. It must be acknowledged, too, that its arguments are exceedingly specious. An answer, however, there is to these arguments, and it can scarcely be thought out of place, that in the life of a Cistercian Saint, some pages should be devoted to a consideration of the subject. Indeed it is in some sort necessary, in order to clear S. Robert from censures, which his manner of life might otherwise draw upon him.

The subject is large, and it will be found difficult to treat of it in few words, but something may be brought forward to show that austerities are not used without a solid reason. Indeed, when it is considered that some of those who have practised lives of great austerity were men of undoubtedly great mind, it is impossible to attribute all this sort of thing to the fanatical devotion of a weak brain. What, then, are the grounds on which have been practised, especially by the Saints, things so repugnant to nature? and what is their object? The grounds lie in the constitution of man's being, and in the fact that he is a fallen creature, having lost by his fall that original integrity in which he was created. The object of austerities is to assist in re-establishing his lost liberty, by breaking up the yoke of fleshly bondage.

Man is a composite being. He is as it were an abridgement of God's creatures. In him are to be found united what God's other creatures possess in solution. He is the link between Spirit and matter. In Him are both: His body is composed of the elements of earth, air, fire, and water. According as these predominate in each individual man, they are the basis of his natural character, whether it be melancholy, volatile, passionate, or phlegmatic. Man, like the rest of the animals, was formed from the ground. But whilst the other animals have each a fixed character, according to their species, man's character varies much in every individual. The first degree of life is that of the vegetable order. This belongs to man, though perhaps difficult to detect. But it is enough that there are instances on record, in which, after death, it has been discovered that the nails and hair have continued to grow. To the vegetable is added in man the animal life. Animals differ from the vegetable order, in their possession of the senses—touch, taste, sight, smell, and hearing.

So far, they are on an equality with man. In this respect, they all fall below him, that man is endued with reason. But allowing to man this great prerogative of reason, which immeasurably exalts him above the rest of the animal creation, still he is of earth, earthy; his lot, like the rest of the animals, commensurate with the duration of his earthly career, his desires and his aims never lifted above the things that pass with time. The designs of God were, however, far higher, as regards this masterpiece of His earthly creation. Man was never intended for a mere inhabitant of earth; he was created with a far nobler destiny. It is true that as far as his body is concerned, it does, like the rest of the animal creation, draw its origin from the earth. God formed Adam from the clay of the ground, not indeed as a dead corpse, but endowed with energetic instincts and activity. If, however, man had been left in this state, though so much excelling the other animals by his reason and lofty capacities, yet his soul, like that of the other animals, being purely of the earth, could never, in this natural order, have aspired to, nor have attained immortality. What is formed of earth must return to earth. If the spark of immortality is to display its splendour in a mortal frame, it must have another origin than earth; it must descend from heaven. This is what we are informed took place in the moment of man's creation. God having formed man, breathed into his soul the breath of life.

In the centre of the animal soul of the first man this mystery took place. God with an indissoluble bond, married to man's animal soul, offspring of the earth, a spiritual principle, emanating from above. Thus were lodged in the same body the spirit, or superior soul, and the psyche, or inferior animal soul. This was effected by that mysterious breathing of God, "and man became a living soul." What God did at His first creation of man, is repeated and continued throughout the whole history of man's race. God, whose fruitfulness is inexhaustible, breathes the breath of life into each of those bodies, which, in the order of nature, is prepared by generation for being animated. Had man held fast his uprightness, and continued in that state of grace, in which he was placed by His Maker, at the moment of his creation, neither he nor his offspring would ever have become the theatre of that intestine war which is carried on within the breast of every child of Adam. The inferior soul would have followed with readiness every movement of the heaven-born spirit; and concord and peace would have been the result. Diversities of character would have still existed, according to the proportion of the different constituent elements in the body of each individual of the human race; that is, of the elements of earth, air, fire, and water.

There would, however, have been no discord between the body and the spirit. But man sinned; and the harmony which previously existed between the different parts of his composite being, was thus disarranged.

The inferior soul no longer kept itself in subjection to the heavenly spirit, but broke the chains, and asserted a lawless liberty. Such is the state of man at this present day. God, it is true, restores men to grace, and regenerates them in His Church; but this regeneration is given to them only as a germ; the fruitfulness of which depends on their own labour and fidelity. It by no means, at once, restores harmony and concord to their being. This must be arrived at by degrees.

Man, being at the same time an earthly and a spiritual being, finds in himself sympathies and attractions, arising from his double nature. The spirit and animal soul, being also so intimately united, cannot but exercise an influence, one over the other. The spirit is drawn down to lend itself to earthly pleasures, desires, and attractions, contrary to its nature; and the animal soul is drawn up to a longing for participation in things above its nature or rightful heritage, namely, the things of immortality. This is the struggle in which every man finds himself engaged. He cannot enfranchise himself from it: it is the law of his nature, earthly and spiritual.

However much he may abandon himself to the desires, affections, and lusts of the earthly part of his being, the spiritual part will renew, at times more or less frequent, a protest against this abasing slavery, and will abhor what she has consented to. She will rise in rebellion; though that rebellion, from the weakness induced by contrary habits, may have no efficacious result. She will pant for God and heaven, and bemoan her bondage to earth, though she have not the courage and strength to break the hated fetters.

But even in those who, by the grace of God, strive to subdue the unruly inclinations of the inferior part of their nature, all have not the same exalted aim; but partly from a faint-hearted cowardice, and partly from want of vocation, the multitude rest content short of having obtained any complete victory. When it is not a question of sin, they permit themselves freely to enjoy the things of earth. The vocation of such is, generally, to live the ordinary life in the world. But whilst they may allowably provide moderate comfort for their body, without luxury, they must not judge those souls, whom God calls to serve Him in cold, and hunger, and want. It is to them an inspiration from on high. It is impossible for a man to enjoy the pleasures of earth, even in moderation, without some detriment to the more noble and spiritual part of his being. Hence he, who would advance in the life of the spirit, must crucify these lower appetites, and endeavour, with the assistance of grace, to bring the earthly element of his being into subjection to the heavenly. This is the object and aim of austerities,—to reconquer the dominion over the body, forfeited by Adam's sin—to spiritualise even the body, if the expression may be used—to enfeeble and starve to death her debased instincts and propensities.

There is no trade which has not its apprenticeship; no art which has not its initiatory principles, its degrees, progress, and perfection. So it is in that art divine and supernatural, in which man is the subject matter, and the artist under the guidance of the Holy Spirit. Christ is the Great Master of this school. He laid down those principles, which have been the basis of the teaching of every other doctor in it. What they have advanced is only the development of the principles He first gave,—the application of them to different classes of men, nations, and climates. Very early in the Church's history systems were formed, the traditions of which, modified according to the character of the period for which they were adapted, have been passed on from age to age, even till this very day.

The first task which the disciple has to undertake is the schooling of his body. He will never be able to live the divine life he is called to, until the body is brought into subjection. For this he endeavours to disengage the organic life from those ties, by which it is shut up in the circle of nature. This result is obtained, first, by reducing the body to the use of those materials which are strictly indispensable to its entertainment; and, secondly, by curtailing the amount of sleep, so as to keep its vital force ever on the stretch. When a severe discipline diminishes the mass of the body, the mind becomes more free and disengaged. The functions of the inferior life, which are vegetable or animal, being less frequently called into action by excitement from without, slacken their operations; and having a smaller amount of materials to assimilate to themselves, they become feebler and feebler. The inferior parts of the body gain greater nervousness and elasticity; the texture of the flesh grows fine and delicate, so as not to impede much the free action of the soul.

When man first tries to fly towards God, he finds himself cumbered and weighed down by the massy envelope of the body. Still, he is under the sad necessity of repairing the losses which his frame is perpetually undergoing. In order, as far as possible, to spiritualise this body, he interdicts to it the use of all such kinds of food as are apt, by their nature, to render it strong and gross; for such diet serves to develop and over-excite the lower functions of man's bodily nature and his animal passions. Its withdrawal leaves his nobler powers free to grow both in extension and intensity, by a concentration of themselves in the soul.

In the vegetable kingdom that aliment has been sought for, which might afford a sufficient nourishment for man, without at the same time over-pressing, by its grossness, the delicate sensibility of his spiritual nature. Two exceptions have been universally allowed in favour of milk and honey. Honey collected principally from flowers, though it perhaps receives some addition in the stomach of the insects which gather it, may be said to be almost wholly vegetable. Milk likewise is almost altogether of a vegetable nature. It resembles, in fact, that oily matter which is produced in the kernel of a fruit, and which is intended to serve for nourishment to the future young plant. Milk in analysis, is composed of oil, mucous matter, and sugar. It contains a very small quantity of azote, which principally characterises the animal life.

It cannot be doubted that matter, in becoming an animal substance, takes, in the change it thus undergoes, a marked character—namely, that of the particular passions, appetites, and instincts of the animal, of whom it has become the substance. These are most probably, at any rate in a measure, transmitted and introduced into the organism of him who feeds upon it. No evil may result from the use of animal food amongst men leading the common life : because in the common life there are sanctioned outlets for the activity of the animal passions.

But if a food, ministering by its organic nature to the nourishment of the animal portion of man's being, were to be made use of by those whose aim is utterly to subdue their lower self, it would render null and void all their efforts. It would perpetuate the struggle, and render the achievement of a victory impossible.

These, then, are some of the reasons for that disciplining of the body, which S. Robert practised, and which has ever been practised by those, who, following the footsteps of the Lord Christ, would live with Him a divine life on the earth. Sometimes this severe discipline is necessary to escape entire reprobation. "I chastise my body, and bring it into subjection, lest, perhaps, when I have preached to others, I myself should become a castaway."

No pharisaical pride must however be taken in these austerities. The following extract from S. Bernard's Apology shows how strongly he reprobates, in Monks, this self-righteous spirit :—

"How," say they, "are those keeping the Rule who are clothed in furs, who when in good health eat flesh, or use dripping; who admit three or four dishes of vegetables on one day, which the Rule forbids; who do no manual labour, which it commands; and in short, according to their pleasure, change, increase, or diminish, many points of the Rule? True. These things cannot be denied. But attend to the rule of God, with which surely the institution of S. Benedict does not disagree. *The kingdom of God is within you*—that is, not external to you, in clothing and aliments of the body, but in the virtues of the interior man. The Apostle also says, 'The kingdom of God is not meat and drink, but righteousness and peace, and joy in the Holy Ghost.' And again: 'The kingdom of God is not in speech but in virtue.' Do ye make up a slander against your brethren with regard to corporal observances? Do ye, leaving the greater matters of the Rule, to wit, its spiritual ordinances, strain out a gnat and swallow a camel? A great abuse, surely! The utmost care is taken that the body be clothed according to the Rule; whilst, contrary to the Rule, the soul is left without its garments, naked. The robe and Cowl must be procured, as if he, who should not have them, were by no means to be esteemed a Monk; and why then are not piety and humility, the spiritual garments, with equal care provided? Clad in robe and full of pride, we abominate furred skins; as if humility clad in furs, were not better than pride clad in a scanty robe; seeing that God himself clothed our first parents in garments of skin; and John in the desert had a girdle of skin about his loins—and the very man, who ordered these robes, yet himself in the solitude wore skins. But with our belly filled to the full with beans, and our mind with pride, we condemn those who are fattened with meats; as if it were not better to make a little use of fat than to be filled to eructation with windy pulse; especially when Esau was chidden, not for eating flesh, but pottage. Adam was not condemned for flesh, but for a fruit tree; and Jonathan was adjudged guilty of death, not for eating flesh, but honey? On the contrary, Elias ate flesh, and it was no hurt to him. Abraham also did what was well pleasing to God when he fed Angels with flesh; and even his own sacrifices God ordained to be of flesh! It is better to use a little wine for infirmity's sake than, with avidity, to swallow down quantities of water. Paul himself counselled Timothy to use a little wine; and our Lord Himself was called a drinker of wine. He gave wine also to His Apostles to drink—nay, He created of it the Sacrament of His Blood. On the contrary, He did not permit water to be drunk at the marriage-feast; and He terribly chastised the murmurings of the people at the waters of strife. David also feared to drink the waters he had longed for. Those men of Gideon's, who drank the water with such avidity as to prostrate in eagerness their whole body, were judged unworthy to go to the battle. And why glory about manual labour, when Martha was chidden for labouring, and Mary praised for being quiet? S. Paul, too, says plainly: 'Labour of the body profiteth little, but piety is profitable for all things.' Surely that labour is the best of which the prophet spoke when he said, 'I have laboured in my groaning,' of which he says in another place: 'I remembered God, and was delighted, and was exercised.' And lest here you should understand bodily exercise, he adds, 'and my spirit waxed faint.' Where the spirit, not the body, is made weary, doubtless a spiritual labour is understood."

CHAPTER IX.

MISSION OF THE CISTERCIAN ORDER.

" The good begun by thee shall onward flow,
In many a branching stream, and wider grow.
The seed that in these few and fleeting hours,
Thy hands unsparing and unwearied sowed,
Shall deck thy grave with amaranthine flowers,
And yield thee fruits in heaven's immortal bowers."
—WILCOX.

NEWMINSTER increased rapidly in numbers under the guidance of its holy Abbot. This Abbey became a mother in five years after its foundation, through the piety of William Buttvillayne, who gave land for the foundation of the Abbey of S. Mary de Divisis, at Pipewell in Northamptonshire. Here it was that Richard Cœur de Lion, at the beginning of his reign, before setting out to the Holy Land, held a council of nobility and clergy, with Baldwin, Archbishop of Canterbury, at their head.

In 1147, Robert also sent forth two other colonies, one to commence the Abbey of Salley in Craven, not far from his own birth-place. The Rectory of Gargrave was afterwards made over to this Abbey, which had for its founder William de Percie.

The third Abbey, founded about the same time, was that of Roche in the south of Yorkshire, not far from Rotherham. One thing which rendered this Abbey famous, and a place of pilgrimage, was that among the fantastical forms, which portions of the fractured limestone had assumed, there was discovered what bore a striking resemblance to the Saviour, stretched on the cross. This natural image was held in high veneration, and visited in pilgrimage by the devout, under the title of our Saviour of the Roche.

Thus S. Robert, from his new Monastery, founded no fewer than three houses in the space of ten years. This was but a sample of the general and rapid growth of the Cistercian Order. It was now but about fifty years from its first commencement, and already it numbered five hundred Abbeys. Its rise and establishment was not after the working of man, but was brought about by the operation of the Holy Ghost. "Who hath ever heard such a thing," says Isaias the prophet, "or who hath seen the like to this? Shall the earth bring forth in one day, or shall a nation be born at once?" To Cîteaux which, not fifty years back, was seemingly on the point of dying in unfruitfulness, it was now said, as by the same prophet, "Lift up thine eyes round about and see. All these are gathered together, they are come to thee. Thou shalt be clothed with all these, as with an ornament;

and, as a bride, thou shalt put them about thee. The children of thy barrenness shall still say in thine ears, 'The place is too strait for me, make me room to dwell in.' And thou shalt say in thy heart, 'Who hath begotten me these? I was barren, and brought not forth; led away and captive; and who hath brought up these? I was destitute and alone, and these, where were they?' Thus saith the Lord God, 'Behold, I will lift up my hand unto the Gentiles, and will set up my standard to the people, and they shall bring thy sons in their arms, and thy daughters upon their shoulders, and kings shall be thy nursing fathers, and queens thy nurses.'"

These words, spoken primarily of the Church, were, in a significant manner, made true also to the Cistercian Order. He, who holds the hearts of all men in His hand, and turns them whithersoever He wills, had previously been busy by the particular visitations of His grace. He had touched many hearts in places and countries far apart, by a simultaneous movement. He had inspired them beforehand with the same sentiments, longings, and ideas. They were waiting in expectation for the sign—burning with vehement desire for its manifestation. When, therefore, the Cistercian Order appeared, it found a multitude ready for it in every land; in East, and West, and North, and South. They gathered themselves together at the whisper of the Spirit; for the Spirit of the Lord had descended, and filled the earth. The Cistercian

Order had but to store up in its garners those who had been already made ripe for it by His interior operations. They felt, they thought, they spoke the same thing; not taught by flesh and blood, or by any earthly communication of sentiment, but moved by Him "who maketh men to be of one mind in an house." The Cistercian Order was the embodiment and expression of ideas, the realisation of which they had hardly dared to hope for. Looking to it as their home, they could say with satisfaction, "This is the place of my rest, here will I dwell, for I have a delight therein."

And as when the Lord of old passed through the land of Egypt, there was not a house in which He left not one dead; so now, as He passed through the Egypt of the world, it might be said, there was not a house, in which there was not one dead; dead, that is to the world, but alive to God. Yes; by His intimate visitation, the Spirit smote down His chosen ones in every house. He respected neither high nor low. The prince and the peasant, the Baron and the serf, became a prey to this soul-subduing influence, which captivated them. Drawn sometimes, as it were, against their will, yet with their will, they bent their necks to the yoke. Out of the most unlikely places, and in the most unlooked-for manner, men came to swell the ranks of the Cistercian family. In the pride of youth, and in the decrepitude of age, the fierce soldier, the mighty statesman, the noblest and most learned, alike with the low and ignorant, gave themselves up as subjects to the Cistercian Rule. Thus it was that the first houses were rapidly filled. They soon became dotted here and here over the whole of Europe. They carried the infection of their ideas wherever they went. Each Abbey became a new centre of their work. Thus they became the leaven of the world, and of all society, so that their historian says of those days, " *Omnia Cistercium erat.*"

There are many different points of view, from which the work of the Cistercian Order may be regarded, and many different phases of it present themselves to one, who would examine it. There are some Apologists of the Order, in the present day, who maintain strongly, that the Cistercians were the great introducers of an improved system of agriculture; that they drained marshy land, rendered desert places and uncultivated forests, fertile and beautiful. For this it is argued, that they are not only not worthy of contempt, but ought to be looked up to with gratitude, as forwarders of the progress of humanity, and benefactors of the human family. Alas! how low is man fallen, how degraded he is become; when recourse must be had to such arguments as these for the defence of the Cistercian Order. The lowest material interests must be appealed to, to obtain any response from an age that is sunk almost to a level with the brutes. Yes, again, it is said, these great Monastic Communities by a life of celibacy, solved the problem, as to what the state must do with her surplus population. These, indeed, are low views. It is melancholy to think, that there should exist men on the face of the earth, to whom no other arguments are a response.

In another point of view, the Cistercian work was the levelling, in a great measure, of the distinction between the noble and the serf—the distinction of classes. By the institution of lay brethren, who were not bound to choir duties, S. Stephen was enabled to admit into his Order numbers of men, in the lower walks of life, who would never, otherwise, have had an opportunity of embracing the Monastic state. The lay brethren, for the most part, were from the serfs, the unfortunate population of the country places; whose life was so full of hardship and discomfort, that, far from finding that of a Monastery more austere, they experienced oftentimes a great amelioration of their former condition. There were, indeed, not wanting altogether, persons of a higher class, who preferred the lay brothers' life as safer, and chose it from high and holy motives, as more conducive to sanctification. Thus the celebrated Doctor of the Schools, Alan, ended his life as a Cistercian lay brother. Sometimes Clergy in holy Orders, hiding their sacred character, and shunning the honours paid to them on that account, would be found concealing themselves also among the ranks of the lay brethren. As a general rule, however, the lay brethren were from the serfs. Not being capable, from want of education, of undertaking the laborious duties of the Choir, in performing the Divine Office, a longer amount of time was spent by them in manual work, to make up for this deficiency. But the Monks of the Choir, when released from those duties, took part of the common labours of the Monastery, according to their strength and capacity. Thus the serf and the noble found themselves, as it were, on an equality. The noble had no delicacies or dainties at the table, but all were fed from the same dishes. Each had the same hard straw mattress, to lie on at night; and all were clothed alike, from the same coarse gray cloth; for it was not till in 1269 that the white Cowl was ordered to be worn by the Choir Monks, and this only during the Divine Office. The gray or brown colour was, for the first time, assigned to the lay brothers as a distinctive mark in 1466. Thus was equality then meted to all. "You had neither shoes nor stockings," said S. Bernard to a dying lay brother, who appeared to show over-confidence, and a somewhat of trust, in the merits of a good life; "you had neither shoes nor stockings; you walked half naked, tormented with hunger and cold, when you took refuge amongst us; and your prayers and supplications had at last obtained for you an entrance; and since then you have been put on an equality as to food, clothing, and all things else, with the learned men and with the height of the nobility who are with us."

Yes, so it was, men occupying the highest positions in society, abandoned the brilliant career on which they were entering, or in which they were already engaged, to live in abject poverty, by the toil of their own hands, like the lowest classes of the nation. The lowest menial offices were equally the lot of learned and unlearned men, rich and poor, noble and serf. "Your brother," it was said to Louis, the King of France, "washes the spoons and dishes in the kitchen of Clairvaux."

Amadeus, who was of a noble French family—indeed of princely blood and delicately nurtured—was discovered by a friend on a visit to him greasing with a stinking mixture of fat and rancid oil the shoes of the Community. S. Bernard himself, when he was Abbot, used to grease his own shoes with the same kind of composition. Once, it is said, the devil, under the disguise of a guest, came into the calefactory, where he was employed, and asked where the Abbot was. The Saint lifted his eyes, and looked at him. "What an Abbot," cried the demon, "would it not be better to be entertaining the guests, than to be disgracing the Monks, by being occupied in such servile and unbecoming employment?" The Abbot continued his work; and the devil disappeared in confusion. In the harvest time, all, without distinction of persons, passed almost the entire day, in the labours of gathering in the produce of the land. At those times the Divine

Office was not chanted, that, freed from its labour, the Monks might devote all their time to that of the field. Thus the dream of the Chartist was realised, on a pretty large scale, when the gentleman and the peasant were seen together at the common labour.

Now this could not be without its effect on the world without. In those times, it may be said, there was no family of any distinction, who had not given some one of its members to the Cistercian Order. The Order became thus a bond of relationship between noble and serf; because the son of the noble, and the son of the serf, in that Order, were brethren. Some proud ones indeed there were, who, when any member of their family joined the Order, were highly indignant. They esteemed it a disgrace to their noble blood that a relation of theirs should lower himself to be the brother of serfs.

When S. Waltheof joined the Abbey of Wardon in Bedfordshire, his brother Simon, Earl of Northampton, whose estates were not far off, sent word that if the Monks did not expel him, he would come and burn the Abbey over their heads. And afterwards, when S. Waltheof was Abbot of Melrose, and went on some business to Stephen, king of England, whose cousin he was, Simon, who happened to be present, and saw him coming, thus spake to the King: "See my Lord King," said he, "how my brother and thy kinsman does honour to his lineage." For Waltheof, in his gray cowl, cut but a mean figure amongst the nobles, clad in rich dresses, and burnished armour. Stephen, however, had not the same proud spirit as the Earl. He could not but admire the Abbot after all. "By God's faith," he answered, "if thou and I had only the grace to see it, he is an honour to us: he is an ornament to our race, as the jewel adorns the gold in which it is set." Then, coming forward, he kissed the Abbot's hand, and bent his head low, for a blessing; granting gladly the petition made of him.

But it is impossible to characterise in two or three points the Cistercian work. They were in fact protesters against all the ills and abuses under which Christendom groaned; the simony and incontinence of the Clergy; the worldly pomp which the Bishops, and even Abbots affected; the unrestrained luxury, violence, bloodshed, and open sins of the laity; the usurpation of Kings in the matter of investitures; and all other vices which rode rampant over Christ's people. Their protest came with overwhelming force, because, by their own austere examples, they showed themselves to have utterly reprobated the vices they sought to extirpate in others. Their actions preached more loudly than their words. Freed from the fetters of the world, its example did not overawe them.

It may be imagined that being removed into solitary places, they would be unable to use much influence on the world. But notwithstanding their solitude, they had certain means of communicating with the world. As Simon Stylites, on his pillar, had an audience of thousands daily, to whom he preached the word of life, so the Cistercian houses were never without their guests; and it was greatly by means of the hostelry or guest-house, that they made head against the prevalent evils of the times. Many, indeed, having entered their houses merely for a night, never again left them. Thus it is said that Otho, the grandson of the Emperor of Germany, with twelve young nobles, fellow-students, came to pass the night at Morimond; and they were so struck and enchanted, that they all remained to embrace the Cistercian mode of life. But many more, who had come on a passing visit or for a pious retreat of a few days, went back into the world changed men; and carrying away with him the Cistercian view of things. For the Cistercians were, many of them, men of great intelligence, who took a lively interest in all the leading questions of the day. It was impossible, therefore, that their views, even as men of mind, should be without their influence on those who came in contact with them. But over and above this natural influence of mind over mind, there was superadded the high respect, paid in the ages of faith, to men who had left the world. For they were esteemed to have clearer views as to what is right or wrong in the judgment of God.

It has been seen how largely the Cistercian ranks were recruited from the highest classes of society; and that which drew into the austere poverty of the Order so many rich and noble persons, attracted also the admiration, and won the sympathy of innumerable others, who were not called to the Monastic life.

It is from the attraction of extremes that the most austere Orders count, amongst their friends and benefactors, so many who move in the highest circles of the world. Those who had around them every luxury, whose career in the world was one of brilliancy and honour, were yet enraptured with Cistercian poverty, and paid homage to the Monk. By their influence over the rich and noble, they propagated the spirit of the Crusades, which, though they gained not all their object, at least saved Europe from the desolation of the Mohammedan yoke. In an anecdote, told of Richard Cœur de Lion, we see the feeling of the times. Richard, being tossed about several hours by a tempest at sea, and in great danger of shipwreck, cried out, "When will the hour come, when the gray Monks rise to praise God? assuredly they will pray for me, who have been such a benefactor to them, and God will save us." And so indeed, at the second hour of the night, the commencement of the Cistercian Vigils, the storm sensibly abated; and there was a calm.

The Cistercian Order was the instrument God employed, for the regeneration of the corrupted society of Christendom. The words spoken to the prophet Jeremiah are of apt application to this Order. "Lo," says God, "I have set thee, this day, over nations, and over kingdoms; to root up, and to pull down; and to waste, and to plant, and to build."

In external appearance, no manner of life could have been so ill adapted for influence over the world as the Cistercian. To an ordinary eye they were a set of pious agriculturists. The primitive design of their Institution was retirement from the world; and all their Monasteries were for this reason built in solitary places. But because, like Solomon, they had sought the heavenly wisdom, God was pleased to add that which they had not sought, riches, honours, and power. It is a remark of a celebrated writer, that "some are born great, others become so by their laborious efforts; and others again have greatness thrust upon them." This last event was the case of the Cistercian Order.

The Cistercian Order became the organ of certain opinions, and principles of action. Its different Monasteries were the machinery for diffusing them. Nothing could be better suited for this purpose, for they were like a net-work spread over the face, not of England only, but of all Europe. Freemasonry has its lodges and its different circles, which correspond with one centre for the propagation of evil; so the Cistercian Order became, without seeking it, in the same manner, an instrument for the propagation of good.

Thus, in the midst of their quiet and stillness, they worked the regeneration of European society. It was not by power of argument, of preaching, or discussion, that they fulfilled their task, but rather their "strength" was in "sitting still." They went not forth against the world with a sword, and with a spear, and with a shield. The weapons of their warfare were not carnal, though mighty in God to the pulling down of fortifications. They rather resembled Him, of whom it was said, "He shall not contend nor cry out, neither shall any man hear His voice in the streets. The bruised reed He shall not break, and the smoking flax He shall not extinguish, till He send forth judgment unto victory." There was nothing brilliant or grand about them, to take the eye, and draw down the esteem of the world. On the contrary, they were the "most abject of men, whose look was, as it were, hidden and despised." For this very reason, it was given them from above "to divide the spoils of the strong," to "see a long-lived seed," and "that the work of the Lord should prosper in their hand."

CHAPTER X.

THE FRIENDS OF S. ROBERT—HIS DEATH AND ASSUMPTION TO BLISS.

> "*He lifts me to the golden doors,*
> *The flashes come and go;*
> *All heaven bursts her starry floors,*
> *And strews her lights below;*
> *And deepens on and up, the gates*
> *Roll back, and far within,*
> *For me the heavenly Bridegroom waits,*
> *To make me pure from sin.*"
> —TENNYSON.

NOW the arch Enemy of souls saw with indignation the havoc that Robert was making in his army, and the losses he had sustained of late years on account of this man. He determined, therefore, to spare no effort for his destruction. This he thought might best be brought about by bringing his name into evil repute through slander and calumny. He laid his snare in the following manner: There was a certain noble lady, whose abode lay at no great distance from Newminster, and who lived in great pomp, surrounded by all the delights and pleasures of this world. This lady, moved by the exhortations of the Saint, set about the commencement of a wholly different life. Renouncing these delusive enjoyments, which deceive worldlings, she gave herself up to the pursuit of the things of the kingdom of God. Amidst all the grandeur of her state, she lived, as it were, the life of a solitary; hating the pride of life, and being poor in spirit.

Now as it came to pass, from time to time, that Robert visited this godly matron, to encourage her by his advice and counsel; this evil and malignant Enemy whispered to some of the Brethren, that it was for no good purpose that Robert paid his accustomed visits, but that his heart had got entangled with an unlawful love; that he was thus feeding its flames, and might soon bring upon the Monastery some notable scandal. These Brethren, inflamed with zeal, as they thought, for the good of the Abbot, and of their Monastery, began to spread abroad and communicate to others their evil suspicions. Under this specious pretext of good, the devil wished to sow division in the Monastery, and so bring to nought the good work which S. Robert was effecting. At last complaints were even brought to the ears of S. Bernard himself. Whether S. Bernard sent for Robert to clear himself, or whether Robert himself thought fit to go, does not appear. Perhaps he only went at that time, because of the sitting of the General Chapter. For by rule the English Abbots had to attend the General Chapter every four years. This last surmise seems the most probable, as it is said that Robert's name and merits were made known to S. Bernard by divine revelation; and that taking him aside he said to him, " Brother Robert, all those things which an evil-minded suspicion hath spread abroad about thee are false."

The date of Robert's journey into France is not mentioned; but as it is said that he met the Pope Eugenius III., it is plain that the year must have been 1148. In this year there was a famous General Chapter over which this Pope, who had been himself a Cistercian Abbot, presided. Eugenius continued to keep up his austerities in the palace of the Vatican, wore his course habit under his pontifical vestments, and lay on a pallet of straw, instead of the grand bed of state. It was at this Chapter that the Savignian Order, comprising thirty Monasteries, of which the famous house of La Trappe was one, received admission into that of Cîteaux. This Order was a reform of the Benedictine founded by S. Vitalis, a disciple of B. Robert of Arbrissel, in the forest of Savigni in Normandy, in 1112. S. Bernard honoured Robert with great marks of affection; and, in token of his conviction, that the charges brought against him were utterly unworthy of credit, he gave to him his own girdle, the emblem of chastity. By this girdle were many miracles afterwards wrought, through the united merits of the two Saints.

Thus Robert came out of the persecution raised

against him with a halo of glory; and those things which had seemed on the point of bringing about his downfall, raised him to greater honour than before. Robert then returned back to Newminster, full of joy. As for his enemies, he did not give them even a word of reproach.

In order to preserve strict discipline, and to keep the whole Cistercian body connected together, it was decreed that the Abbot of any Mother house, should make every year a formal visitation of all Abbeys founded by it. During one of S. Roberts journeys as he passed through Newcastle, he saw the Enemy of souls, disguised under the appearance of a gay cavalier, and very busy exciting a quarrel amongst the citizens. Robert seeing it to be a wicked devil under the guise of a man, ordered him to follow him out of the town, where, having made him confess who he was, and what he was about, he sent him off into the desert, bidding him never more to dare to tempt mankind.

The wicked spirit obeyed, but left at his departure such a stench of brimstone, that the horses, neighing, and snorting, and pawing the ground, could scarcely be kept in control by their riders. God discovered also to His servant one day, when celebrating the holy Mysteries, the destruction of a vessel at sea. He saw it dashed against a rock, broken to pieces, and then swallowed up, with all the men on board. Moved by compassion, he signified the spot to his Monks, who went to the sea shore, gathered up the bodies of the drowned, and gave them Christian burial.

Robert was joined in the intimacy of a holy friendship, as well with S. Godrick, as with S. Bernard. S. Godrick lived at Finchale hermitage, three miles from Durham, near the river Were, and about twenty miles from Newminster. Here he passed a solitary life, given up to holy exercises and prayer. He was not in any Ecclesiastical Orders. When Surius, therefore, in his life of S. Robert, says that he used to make his confessions to S. Godrick, this is a mistake. Still, however, Robert used to consult his friend in all spiritual matters, since, though not endowed with human learning, he yet had the science of the Saints, which being infused directly into the soul by God, is a much more excellent kind of knowledge. They therefore sometimes would shut themselves up together, and pass long hours in divine entertainments, concerning the things of the kingdom of God. In these conversations they found such wonderful comfort and consolation, that the hours so spent appeared to them like fruit stolen from the trees of paradise.

S. Godrick had known Robert when he was at Whitby, for there this same Saint had led a hermit's life for a year and some months.

When, therefore, Robert came to Newminster, the old friendship was renewed, and became cemented into a closer union of love. As he was returning from the General Chapter of his Order, which was held at Cîteaux, he came as was his wont to the holy hermit, to receive from him some word of consolation. For, indeed, he oftentimes turned aside from the way for this purpose. S. Godrick had been fifty years an inmate of his hermitage; and though he was now lying in extreme weakness on his bed, which he never left, yet his mind rose above his body, and he was endowed with many supernatural gifts; knowing often of events which happened a great distance off, as clearly as though he were present.

He had also the gift of prophecy. When therefore Robert was taking his leave, he said to him, as the tears rose into his eyes, conjuring and imploring him: "I beseech thee, O my Lord, and Reverend Father, not to forget thy fellow-servant; for, of a surety, thou wilt never again behold him in the corruption of this mortality." These words Robert recollected, and, before his end, he said to a certain Monk, his near relation, as he stood by him, "I know that God is about to deliver me to this transitory death; for this Godrick, the man of God, clearly signified to me."

Robert then returned home, and on the Saturday after Ascension fell grievously ill. From that day, to the time of his death, he was pressed with continual sickness. When he had received the holy Viaticum, and was evidently dying, some ancients of the Brethren desired to know of him, who he considered fittest to be his successor. The dying Saint acceded to their wish, in naming one of the Brethren; knowing nevertheless, with prophetic instinct, that his counsel would not be taken. "I know well," he said, "ye will not follow my advice, but elect Brother Walter;" and so indeed it befell after his death that they rejected his counsel. Soon after this he raised his hands to heaven, and prayed for his spiritual sons and for his Monastery, and so passed away to his reward. The Cistercian Order keeps his festival on the seventh of June, which, in the year 1159, was the day of his happy departure. His name also occurs on this day, in all the martyrologies of the west.

"It was," says Reginald the Monk of Durham, "as the twilight of Saturday night was setting in, that the spirit of the Abbot was loosed from the flesh, and his soul, seeking for heaven, returned to Him who had given it to the body. It was that Saturday, which falls within Pentecost, and is called the Saturday of jubilee, for this reason, because at that moment of time, by the gift and grace of the Holy Ghost, remission of sins is imparted to the faithful, and in very truth, the moment of that time, then pressing on, was a certain oracular, and heavenly presage, and a seal of that eternal blessedness which was laid up in store for him. The Abbot underwent the penalty of death, but, by undergoing this transitory death, he purchased the sweetness of eternal life. For, having put off the shroud of this mortality, he was, by the mercy of God, associated to the choir of the Angelic Spirits. The venerable company of his Monks gathered round him, when the hour that he should depart to his home drew nigh. They bid him a last farewell, commending by pious prayers and litanies the spirit of their Father to the Lord, and beseeching the Angels to come to his assistance, and take him with them to the heavenly court."

And indeed that the Angels should eagerly accept the invitation was not to be wondered at, inasmuch as, even whilst held by this corruptible life, Robert had become their companion in singing the praises of God. For it cannot be doubted that the Angels take special interest in those who sing the holy psalmody, in the choirs of the Church upon earth. Sometimes it happened that, even before the veil of flesh had been rent asunder, the Cistercian Monks were admitted to the hearing of the psalmody of heaven. Cesarius, in his dialogues of the dying, speaks thus of the priest Meyner:—After matins were accomplished, the Prior went to visit him. "Ah," said he to him, "all night long I was keeping festival. Had I a hundred tongues, I could not unfold the joy of internal gladness which I experienced. I saw the transporting light of God, I heard the celestial harmony, I was present in the choirs of those that sing psalms in heaven. Ah! with what order, with what distinctness, with what reverence, they sang the psalmody. Multitudinous was the number and the character of their voices. But as in a harp, the variety of strings give forth a uniform tune, so did that concordant diversity agree in one melody, delectable beyond the mind of man to conceive. The graver voices sang deep and low, whilst those of the young maidens rose on high making the diapason. And whilst I was wondering at these things, one, who stood by me in venerable apparel, said to me, 'Why marvellest thou? This is the praise of the Word of God.'"

If Robert had not such a glorious vision whilst yet in the body, it is plain from what follows that he was destined immediately on his departure to be admitted to it. Godrick, at that same hour of his dissolution, learned, by a revelation of the Spirit, of the departure of his friend.

Being at prayer in his cell, he was rapt into a transport, and beheld an intense light, penetrating into the darkness of the night. Then there were seen by him two walls of glistening brightness, reaching from earth to heaven, in the midst of which, with a most sweet flight, three Angels ascended up on high. Higher and higher they soared, bearing aloft with them, into the ethereal realms of bliss, the spirit of the holy Abbot. One Angel on his right hand sustained him; another on his left bore him forward; whilst, high above them all, a third led the way, with exceeding jubilant exultation.

The spirit, loosed from the body, had an appearance like to a transparent fiery globe; and, as it were, the semblance of glistening light. As they ascended, the Enemy of the human race met them; but he went back in confusion, for he could find nothing to lay hold of in him. Thus was the soul of the holy man carried into heaven. The gates of heaven opened of their own accord; and lo! a voice was heard, repeating twice: "Enter now, my friends." The spirit meanwhile was welcomed by the companies of the blessed, and surrounded by innumerable cohorts of the heavenly armies. Godrick, with the eye of contemplation, accompanied him throughout his journey; and was transported with exceeding joy of exultation, and most sweet gladness. For he saw him, amidst the escort of the Angels, ascended on high. He assisted at the gladsome spectacle, that he might be a truthful witness of his having attained to the possession of everlasting beatitude. For he saw unlocked to him by the Lord the gates of the heavenly kingdom. "Whence," says Reginald, "when sometimes we importuned him, as to what we ought to think of the spirit of the Abbot, he would answer: 'Would to God that we too were partakers, with him, of the heavenly glory.' One, who is indeed yet in this corruption, saw with his bodily eyes this soul, loosed from the workshop of the flesh, and carried up into the heavens, to enjoy the society of the Angels."

All that night, and the day following, Godrick spent in praising the Divine Goodness. On the following day, after having assisted at the solemnity of the

Adorable Sacrifice, and received the divine life-giving food of the Eucharist, he gave tidings to the priest who assisted him, of the decease of the Abbot, when as yet no announcement had been able to reach them, from so great a distance.

Thus, then, was Robert received into the joy of his Lord. It pleased God that the soul of a holy woman at Hastings, called Edith, should be, at the same moment, taken up into glory. This also was seen by Godrick; and he said it was done, for the greater triumph, and glory, of them both; and for the confusion of the Enemy. Whenever afterwards Godrick spoke of Robert's assumption into bliss, he spoke with such sweetness of compunction, and tears; that all who heard him, felt themselves also to pant, and sigh, with desire of eternal blessedness.

The deceased Abbot was first buried in the Chapter, but so many miracles took place at his tomb, that his body was translated to a more convenient place in the Church.

A blind man there had his sight restored to him; a lunatic was brought back to the full use of reason; and many received cures of different bodily maladies. A certain man, who was deaf and dumb from his mother's womb, had for a long time implored the assistance of S. Thomas of Canterbury. At length the holy Martyr appeared to him, and bade him with all speed proceed to Newminster, where, by the relics of S. Robert, he should obtain a perfect cure. But he, murmuring in his own mind, answered, "and who will be my guide during the journey, or provide me with the expenses?" S. Thomas answered, "He will be thy guide, who by a word created all things." The man believed, and going to S. Robert's tomb received with gladness the gifts of speech and hearing.

CHAPTER XI.

DECADENCE OF THE CISTERCIAN ORDER.

> "*The Abbeys and the arches,*
>   *And the old Cathedral piles!*
> *Oh! weep to see the ivy,*
>   *And the grass in all their aisles!*
> *The vaulted roof is fallen,*
>   *And the bat and owl repose,*
> *Where once the people knelt them,*
>   *And the high 'Te Deum' rose.*"
>   —COXE'S "CHRISTIAN BALLADS."

ALAS for Newminster, Fountains, and Clairvaux! All they that go by these venerable places are bewildered with astonishment at the ruin they behold. They see them become the monuments of the wrath of an avenging God. What has happened to them is a lesson to all Monks to keep strictly to the Constitutions and observances of their first Fathers. In the times of the first commencement of the Cistercian Order, it might have been said of her, as of Jerusalem of old, that "her Nazarites were purer than the snow, whiter than milk;" but their face afterwards became "blacker than the coal." Therefore the Lord cast off His altar, and abhorred His sanctuary. He gave up into the hand of the enemy the walls of her palaces: her gates are sunk into the ground. All they that go by clap their hands, saying, " Is this that which was called the perfection of beauty, the joy of the whole earth ?"

" Let us sit and weep," says S. Augustine, "remembering Sion; for many weep with Babylonian tears, who also rejoice with Babylonian joy. They rejoice in gain and weep at losses, and both of Babylon. We ought to weep from remembering Sion. The waters of Babylon flow and pass; let us weep by them. But beware how we enter them, lest we be borne away by them and swallowed up in them. Let us sit by them and weep; and we shall weep if we remember Sion." Jeremiah wept over the stones of Jerusalem. It is for us to weep over the stones of the sanctuaries of ancient days.

Newminster lies flat with the ground,—a funeral monument of its sainted founder. His body rests beneath the mouldered pile. For though the Ballandist life of him says, that a Westphalian Monastery professes to have some portion of his reliques, no translation of his *body*, it is very certain, ever took place.

Nothing remains of the Abbey but the archway of the door of the Church. All is green sward, overspreading long lines of walls, and irregular heaps of ruins. The Church stood on ground considerably higher than the level of the plain which surrounds it. It was on the north side of the Abbey, and consisted of a tower, nave, transept, and chancel; in all, about 270 feet long. The cloisters were on the south side of the Nave, about 102 feet from east to west, and 80 feet from north to south, and had extensive buildings on each side of them. The Chapter-house, and many other smaller buildings, of various sizes, lay on the east and south. From this side to the north wall of the Nave of the Church, the ruins cover about 320 feet.

Some large ash-trees and hawthorn, and abundance of wake-robin, grow in these ruins. Under a group of ash-trees, to the south-west of the Abbey, a fine spring rises out of a gentle knoll, on which are traces of masonry. This water was probably conveyed hither in a covered conduit; and a narrow marsh, a sort of natural fosse, sweeps between it and the banks, round three sides of the Abbey. So much for Newminster. The beautiful ruins of Fountains Abbey are famous everywhere. These majestic piles were not the buildings of the first Cistercians. They are the product of a later period, when the Order began to decline from that austere poverty which characterised the first Cistercian edifices.

Whilst we admire, we should also lament; because the majesty of these piles shows forth the decay of the internal spirit of the Order.

We read in the life of S. Wolfstan, Bishop of Wigorne, that, in his time, they threw down the simple Cathedral, which S. Oswald had built, and erected in its place a magnificent Church. S. Wolfstan, however, far from being pleased at the sight, wept with grief. Ah, said he, see how we overthrow the works of the Saints, that we may get glory before men! They knew how to make a sacrifice of themselves to God in any sort of buildings; and they drew others to their example. We, on the contrary, neglecting the care of the soul, heap up stones.

But though the magnificence of Fountains Abbey is not altogether in keeping with the rule of Cîteaux, yet who can believe that those, who erected these structures, were men sunk in the darkest ignorance, and the grossest superstition? No. It can never be. The genius and imagination, that could conceive such sublime works of art, as these men have left behind them, must have been of no vulgar stamp.

With all the boasted light and intelligence of the present day, architects yet feel quite flattered, if what they can produce may bear some comparison with the past. The men of those times, ignorant of metaphysical theories, so blended forms and magnitudes, as to produce the artificial infinite, and the real sublime. They erected temples to God, which seem intended to rival in durability the earth, on which they stand, and which, after the lapse of ages, are still unequalled, not only for magnificence of structure, but in their tendency to dilate the mind; and to leave upon the soul the most solemn and deep impressions. Indeed, these structures of Christian art bear, on their face, the reflection of a supernatural beauty, which wraps up on high the astonished and bewildered mind. And it is difficult adequately to account for this phenomenon, except by supposing, that the conception itself of these buildings was an inspiration from above. For the imagination, acted on by the Spirit of God, is transported beyond the ordinary circle of its power, and rises into a higher sphere, where it receives impressions above what it is naturally capable of attaining to. The ideal type of infinite beauty and holiness is, in a measure, unfolded to its view: and the works of the Christian artist are an endeavour to express, and manifest, in some sensible external form, the noble conceptions thus generated within. It is for this reason they have the effect of elevating the minds of those who behold them. Although they fall short of the ideal type whose excellence is their model, yet they are far exalted above all the efforts of mere natural genius.

Clairvaux is still in being. It is not now, as S. Bernard jestingly called it, an open prison, but it is a prison of the state; a Monastery it is true, but one in which all the inmates are detained against their will. Otherwise, the discipline does not vary so very much from that of the ancient Cistercian Rule. The successors of the Monks sleep longer than the followers of S. Bernard. They have ten hours in winter, eight and a half in summer. But then their work lasts eleven or twelve hours in the day; that of the Monks with their choir duties not more than ten. They have two meals each day, and on four days of the week may have meat, if they have laboured well; so that in this respect they are less strict than their predecessors. The colour of their garments is the same as that of the ancient Cistercians, gray; though it differs in form. They keep a continual silence, but a silence of coercion, instead of one of choice. A soldier with sword at his side enforces its observance. The Chapter is still the place for punishment of faults, but not of the fraternal corrections of the olden time. All is done now by force. The successors of the Monks live celibate by compulsion, they are poor by compulsion, obedient by compulsion, silent by compulsion. They pray, or seem to pray, at certain hours, and on certain days, because compelled so to do. Clairvaux ought to receive back its old name, "the valley of Wormwood."

Clairvaux, S. Bernard's own Abbey, is therefore now a common prison. The ruins of Fountains are a resort for idle or curious sight-seers. Newminster is levelled to the ground. We stand astonished, we are amazed, and bewildered! What has been the cause of so great a destruction? Surely there must have been some deep reason, why it has been per-

Decadence of the Cistercian Order. 153

mitted that the whirlwind should, with such violence, sweep away these Institutions, once so full of the beauty of holiness. Can it be for a moment supposed, that God would have permitted the ruthless hands of iniquity to spoil His Sanctuaries, and work so complete a ruin of them, had not their inmates first forsaken their allegiance to Him, been false to the vows of their holy profession, and turned their backs upon the traditions of their Fathers? No! so long as they were faithful, they enjoyed the protection of God, and the esteem of men. For, when a man's ways please the Lord, He maketh even his enemies to be at peace with him. But there came a time when the Cistercians forgot their first love. Then came a softening of the too great rigour, as it was thought, of the Rule;—a relaxation, little by little, of the bands of the ancient discipline;—and so things went on, till, two hundred years after its commencement, matters had come to such a pass, that it required the hand of a Pope, to reform the Order.

But of what value is a reform, forced upon unwilling hearts? The Order went on decaying, till all the ancient spirit was gone: and as its spirit waned, its members wasted away in a like proportion; so that Clairvaux, which in the time of S. Bernard had eight hundred Monks, had at the time of its dissolution in 1790, only a Community of thirty-six. Fountains at its dissolution, had about thirty; and Newminster, but fifteen.

Astonishing thing! So long as the Cistercian Monasteries preserved that austerity, poverty, and simplicity, which so characterised them in their primitive fervour, then bad vocations were rare; and such was the vast number of Novices, which flowed from all sides into the Order, that Clairvaux alone in S. Bernard's time became mother of one hundred and sixty houses. But, when they allowed worldliness and relaxations to creep into their Cloisters, the number of Monks began to dwindle away; so that although it was a rule, that no Abbey should have fewer than thirteen Monks, inclusive of the Abbot, we find in England Abbeys, with a community of three, and even only two Monks; so true it is, that every institution which turns away from the fulfilment of its primitive aim and object becomes blasted, and is struck with a death-stroke, by a sentence of Providence. God's blessing is in an inexplicable manner tied up with the exact observation of what may seem but very trifles. As the secret of Samson's strength lay in his unshorn hair, because by it he was dedicated to God; so the strength of each Religious Order lies in the observance of the principles, given to it by its founders; for they are the peculiar method of its consecration to God. No jealousy can be too great in the guarding of them inviolate. Happy had it been for the Cistercian Order never to have departed from the original purity of its primitive discipline. But love of ease, like another Delilah, caused it to betray and give up its secret source of strength. And when its strength was gone, it became soon after the scorn and mockery of the men of violence, who worked its ruin.

The prodigal munificence of benefactors was one great cause of the ruin of the Cistercian Order. "Give me neither poverty nor riches," says Solomon. If extreme poverty be a hindrance to the Monastic life on account of the cares it engenders, riches are a yet far greater evil. When Constantine the Great gave to S. Sylvester, with so great generosity, all those possessions, whether in or out of the City of Rome, to enrich the Church; some persons recount that a voice was heard to say, others that a hand was seen writing, "*Hodie venenum infusum est Ecclesiæ.*" But with more probability is it reported, that, when the Countess Mathilda by her will, in the time of Gregory VII., gave the lands, now called the patrimony of S. Peter; a voice was heard to say, "*Venenum melle litum fœminam Christianis propinasse,*" (see Theatr. Vitæ: Hum. p. 131.) Such a cup of poison, disguised in honey, did certain so-called benefactors give to their Cistercian clients; making the breach of the Rule the very condition of their accepting the proffered favours. It has been seen in a former chapter, that the Cistercians rejected in matter of food and the number of dishes all that was not in strict accordance with S. Benedict's Rule. Two kinds of dishes were alone allowed; and these even at Easter were supplied to the primitive Cistercians from the field or garden. But as Peter asked the Lord to spare Himself the sufferings he was predicting, because he yet savoured the things of this world, and was thus a Satan to his Lord, so did these kind benefactors ask the Cistercians to spare themselves, and depart a little from that rigour of their Rule;—indulge a little the desires of the fleshly appetite;—and the poor Monks fell into the trap, laid for them by these smooth-spoken adversaries.

It was the practice at Clugni to give, over and above the two dishes allowed by S. Benedict, extra food of a better quality, under the name of pittances! These divers kinds of food were, however, rejected by the Cistercians; and were only allowed, in case of real necessity, to the more weakly of the Brethren. But certain persons made donations, and even left in their wills sums of money, on condition that they should be employed, in the obtaining of pittances for the Monks. In the very time of S. Bernard, 1152, we find Gaultier, Count of Brienne, giving to Clairvaux a yearly rent of a hundred sous, to be laid out in a pittance, once a year, for all the Monks in general. This is the first registered instance of the kind. In 1175 Louis VII. gave a yearly sum of thirty livres sterling to Clairvaux, to be employed in buying six pittances, the half to be given at Easter, the other half at Christmas. The practice of giving money for pittances soon grew up into a system; and Monks used even to ask the friends of their Abbey to bestow their alms in the shape of a pittance.

In the fourteenth century the right of pittances on certain Feast-days was acknowledged by the general Chapter; and the prohibition to the Abbot to give pittances three days running is no longer renewed. In the beginning of the thirteenth century the Monks in many places began to season their vegetables also with butter and oil; and later on, flesh meat was eaten by some, on pretence of special dispensations from the Pope. When Benedict XIV. reformed the Order, one of the things he particularises, is the withdrawal of all licences to eat flesh-meat. By this reform several houses were violently cut off from the Order. In certain Abbeys an officer called "pittanciarius," was appointed by the Monks, who gave out pittances without asking the Abbot's consent. It seems evident that such an officer, appointed in violation of the Rule, existed at Clairvaux so early as 1260. In 1289 the General Chapter decreed the suppression of all such officers; but there was something more than a decree of the Chapter required, to call back the spirit of S. Stephen and S. Bernard; and the Order continued its downward course till its houses were violently suppressed by the State.

Another custom also had been introduced rather early, which the Editor of the "Monasticon Cisterciense" in vain tries to palliate, as not contrary to the Rule; this was that of the whole Community going to the Refectory after None or Vespers, according to the time of year, to drink a certain part of their allowance of wine. It was to be expected what this would ultimately lead to, namely, the introduction of a second meal throughout the year.

Side by side with these relaxations in diet, is to be seen a declension in the simplicity of Church ornaments. During the first days of the Order, the usage of ornaments of silk was prohibited, both to Monks and Abbots, even in the most solemn ceremonies. The Cope was never to be worn. In 1152, however, it was permitted to Abbots, to wear Copes of silk, during the ceremony of their benediction; but at no other time. In 1257 permission is given to the Abbot to wear a Cope on all days when he uses the pastoral Staff, and on all days when white is the colour of the day. In 1157 Monks were forbidden to wear Copes or Dalmatics, even when assisting a Bishop at High Mass, in a Church of the Order, but in 1257 it is permitted to Monks, simply assisting their Abbot, to wear Dalmatics and Tunicles. By S. Stephen's regulations the Stole, and Maniples, of the assistant Ministers, were to be only of some common material. They were after a time allowed to be of silk. In 1182 it was still forbidden to have Chasubles of pure silk, but in 1226 Chasubles of silk were fully allowed, if they were not bought by the Abbey, but given to it.

How different was this from the spirit of S. Stephen,

who sent away from the Monastery, ornaments which had been already used there, because he considered them unfitting to the austere poverty, and simplicity, of the kind of life he would profess. It was not the buying of these things, that S. Bernard declaimed against with such vehemence, but the using of them; because, said he, "we Monks have renounced everything that is delectable to the sight." The allowing to be received, as gifts, what the Cistercian constitutions had forbidden to be worn at all, was a plain violation of the constitutions of the Fathers of the Order, and opened the door to all sorts of luxury in Ecclesiastical ornaments.

By means of the liberality of benefactors, the inside appearance of Cistercian Churches was quickly changed. Gilded crosses were allowed by the General Chapter in 1157, if not of large dimensions. By the ancient constitutions no crosses were allowed, except of simple painted wood. In 1256 authorisation is given to dress the altars on grand festivals, with frontals, &c., of pure silk.

Numerous foundations for supplying Monasteries with wax-lights caused the prescriptions of Cîteaux to be set aside on this matter also. The Monastic Churches increased in grandeur, and began to be ornamented with sculpture and expensive marble. Majestic towers were added, instead of the simple wooden belfry, allowed by the constitutions. In 1489 the Abbot of Cîteaux obtained from Innocent

VIII. the power to celebrate Mass pontifically with mitre, ring, and sandals. The ancient spirit of S. Stephen and S. Bernard was then dead. The Abbot was no longer a poor Monk, leading a hidden life, but a magnificent personage, who was the lord of five military Orders, and sat in a lofty chair in the Parliament of Burgundy on a level with the Bishop.

What, perhaps, more than anything else, tended to the complete overthrow of the ancient spirit and discipline of the Order, was the erection of Cistercian Colleges, at the different Universities and seats of learning. The Cistercians were never foes to learning; for we find S. Bernard's brother Nivard placed with a priest, to complete his studies before he should enter the Order. Otho of Freisinghen also, who had rather hastily entered the Noviciate, was sent to Paris even after his profession, to complete his studies; this, too, from Morimond, one of the four Abbeys founded by S. Stephen, and under his control. But, as a general rule, resort was not made to any means of education outside the cloister; and scholastic subtleties were utterly discouraged. But as the Cistercian Order declined in fervour, it declined likewise in the esteem of the world. The Mendicant Orders, and the Dominicans, began to come in for a large share of those favours, hitherto so lavishly bestowed on the Cistercians. What is to be done?

The Order now no longer, as in the olden days, draws into its bosom the learned men of the world.

There is not the same odour of sanctity in the Cloister to attract them. An attempt is, at first, made by a course of studies within the Cloister to compete with these new and formidable rivals; but seeing that the Monks are still in the background, Stephen Lexington, an Englishman, Abbot of Clairvaux, by a bold stroke, clears away the difficulty; and in open violation of the fundamental principles of the Cistercian Reform, forbidding Monasteries to be constructed in towns, founds for his Monks the College of S. Bernard at Paris. This glaring irregularity, contrary to the Chart of Charity, he endeavours to cover by a pontifical dispensation. This happened in 1244. In 1254 the new College is allowed to receive novices, which is an additional derogation from the ancient received maxims of the Order. The number of these Cistercian Colleges soon mounts up to seven; one being at Oxford, called S. Bernard's College, now S. John's, which was founded in the year 1280. It was made obligatory for each Monastery to send subjects. An Abbey having eighteen Monks must send one; having forty Monks, two; and so in proportion. When Monks gave so much time to book-learning, manual labour naturally became distasteful and irksome; as also the coarse food, which hunger, produced by labour, could alone render palatable. Things grew worse and worse till, in 1475, Pope Sextus IV. gave permission to the General Chapter to dispense with the abstinence from flesh meat whenever they thought it necessary. It is not a matter to be wondered at in the then state of the Order, that all Monasteries largely availed themselves of this dispensation. It may be said now, that though the name "Cistercian" was retained, nothing remained of the substance of the life of Cîteaux. No longer fasts of the Order, only those of the Church; and even on those days, an abundant supper. No longer the coarse woollen garb or straw mattress, but shirts of linen and feather beds; no longer any night vigils, but rising at four or five in the morning; no working with the hands, nor silence, nor pious reading, but conversation and idleness;— all day promenading in the courts and gardens; or even hunting and gaming. Such became the state of things (some of the larger Monasteries might be better) when Henry VIII. swept them off from the face of England.

This was God's judgment on their infidelity, though it was a wicked hand which struck the blow. They had been weighed in the balances, and had been found wanting. Their fate is a terrible example of the vengeance of God on all who are unfaithful to the Rule of their Order.

CHAPTER XII.

PAST, PRESENT, AND FUTURE.

" Rise and subdue to thee all as of old,
Those that were true to thee, those that were cold;
Earth, now no home for thee,
Then shall become for thee
One mighty shrine;—
One vast community,
Known by its unity,
Truly divine."
—Songs of Christian Chivalry.

AT the time of the dissolution of the Religious houses, England had one hundred, Ireland seventy Cistercian Abbeys. There were no doubt good and holy Monks, even in those times, but the most of them were Monks only in name.

What right hath thirty men to be living an easy, comfortable life at Fountains, on lands and money, intended by benefactors for those only who kept the hard austere Rule of Cîteaux.

These alms were never given for such a purpose;

the Monks, therefore, of that time were guilty of robbery and sacrilege, in diverting, to their own ease and comfort, possessions dedicated to God. They accepted the gifts, but did not fulfil the obligations, tacitly imposed on them by the donors. It would be well, indeed, if this were all that could be urged against them; but unfortunately there were to be found sometimes instances, in which these so-called Monks, not only violated the rules and constitutions of their Order, but even transgressed against the common obligations of a Christian profession.

In France, and other countries, many reforms of the Order, or portions of it, were set on foot in later times, with more or less of success. The most celebrated and lasting was that of De Rancè in 1664. At the time of the French Revolution in 1790, Dom Augustin saved one house, which took refuge in the Russian dominions. From this a Colony was sent to Lullworth in 1794, where an Abbey was founded. But on the restoration of quiet in France this Community was transferred to Melleraye.

In 1831 the English Monks were expelled from France on a pretext of an obsolete law. They took refuge in Ireland, and were formed into the Community of the Abbey of Mount Melleraye in the County of Waterford.

In 1835 a Colony was sent from thence to form the Abbey of Mount S. Bernard in Leicestershire. This Abbey was founded by the piety of Mr Ambrose

Phillipps de Lisle, Lord of the Manor of Garendon and Grace Dieu.

At Garendon there had formerly been a Cistercian Abbey. It was partly on this account that he desired to see a Cistercian foundation again arise in his neighbourhood. This was effected by the purchase, and donation, of a plot of ground, on the skirts of his patrimonial estate. After so many years, therefore, of exile, the Cistercian Order re-entered a land which had been formerly so hospitable to it. Again, after so many years of silence, was to be heard the solemn chant of a Cistercian choir in its midnight office; and over the wild heaths of the Forest of Charnwood the sound of the prayer-bell calling to office, rung out clear and loud seven times a-day. These industrious Monks soon also brought a great change over the exterior face of nature, in the formerly almost barren spot which they occupied, and, as the Scripture says, "the desert began to blossom as the rose." Instead of the briar came up the fir-tree, and instead of the nettle came up the myrtle-tree; the box-tree, and the pine-tree together, to beautify the place of the sanctuary of the Lord. They began their austere life with a very poor building; but by the charity of various benefactors, especially of the Earl of Shrewsbury, they have been enabled to erect a fair and noble Abbey worthy of their ancient days.

The pious pilgrim, when paying a visit to this

Monastery, is carried back, as it were, to the time of the Middle Ages. The appearance of the Abbey itself, the Monks, apparelled in their long robes, or Cowls; the striking Calvary, which rises on an eminence close by,—are all so utterly different from what he has been used to see, that he can hardly imagine that he is in England of the nineteenth century. He seems to be suddenly brought into collision with England of the olden time.

It remains still a question, how far the Cistercian Rule will find favour in England, and spread its houses throughout the land, as it formerly did. It is plain, however, from the rising of a Benedictine Brotherhood in the Church of England, that the Monastic spirit is not altogether uncongenial to the English Nation in these times; and if only, by the providence of God, England is again brought into communion with the rest of Christendom, there is every probability that the Cistercian Order will flourish in it as of old. The founder of the Cistercian Order, Stephen Harding, was himself an Englishman, so that its rules have doubtless something connatural to the English character.

There are some persons, indeed, who believe that this Order was raised up by God for certain emergencies of the Church, and that now the causes for which He called it into existence are past and gone. These persons, therefore, regard the Order merely as a quaint relic' of ancient times, whose use has ceased, but which may be preserved from absolute destruction on account of the services once rendered by it to religion. Others, on the contrary, consider its Rule, as forming an integral part of the features of the Church's Constitution, which she could not well dispense with. They esteem the observances of the Order to be peculiarly suited for these times of restless utilitarianism, as forming at least some counterbalance to the prevailing spirit of the age. It remains, however, to be seen whether the Cistercian Order is to play any distinguished part in the grand movements of the Church of the future. We are now hastening to the close of another thousand years of the Christian Dispensation. The first thousand years were the period of the purgative life for the Church. The second thousand have been that of her illuminative life. During this illuminative period, many points of doctrine have been cleared by the Church from all doubtfulness, the last crowning act of hers being the definition of the dogma of the Immaculate Conception of Mary.

The intellect, fighting against revealed truth, is rapidly exhausting its subjects. The last article of the Creed, "the life everlasting," is now its grand subject of dispute. The discoveries of science, whilst at first, they seem to teach what is irreconcilable with revelation, yet ultimately end by ranging themselves as additional evidences in her favour. It was only to be expected that, before its final surrender, the untamed intellect of man would make a last and desperate effort to shake off the yoke of subjection to the divine law of faith. This is the cause of that intellectual strife, which, as Schlegel remarks, is the characteristic mark of the present generation, the deepening symptoms of which furnish one more proof that the final day of ultimate decision is approaching.

When reason has consented to take its proper place, being subject to the higher and clearer lights of faith, then shall there be a peace in man's intellectual powers, the fruit of concordant lights. Christianity, having overcome all opposition, will then reign triumphant; this victory being all the more glorious, because preluded by a seeming victory on the part of the powers of evil. He that led into captivity shall be led away captive; he that killed with the sword, shall by the sword himself be slain. Then, says Schlegel, the perfect triumph of divine Revelation, and the fiery baptism of the Spirit, which in those last days shall be administered, shall bring with them the long promised universal peace of the soul, when, under a divine Leader, the Invisible, now become visible, all that hope in Him, of all kindreds and families, shall be reunited in Him in one love and one fellowship.

So great will be the change in the face of all things, that some, says this great philosopher, have actually fallen into the plausible error of regarding this third step of enlightenment as an absolutely new Revelation; whereas it is quite clear that it will be nothing more than a simple completion of the earlier steps.

Then will be fulfilled the last stage of the mystical prophecy of Ezekiel, concerning the holy waters: "He measured a thousand, and he brought me through the water up to the ankles. And again he measured a thousand, and he brought me through the water up to the knees. And he measured a thousand, and he brought me through the water up to the loins. And he measured a thousand, and it was a torrent, which I could not pass over, for the waters were risen, so as to make a deep torrent, which could not be passed over."

It is during this last period, that will take place the perfect fulfilment concerning the triumphs of Christ's kingdom upon earth, when the fulness of the Gentiles shall come in, and the Jews shall bend their neck also to the yoke of faith, according to the prophecy of S. Paul. Of them S. Paul says, that if their rejection has been the reconciliation of the world, what shall the receiving of them be but life from the dead? giving us thereby most glorious things to expect, at the epoch of their conversion.

During this unitive period of the Church's life, S. Bonaventure says, that as far as is possible, whilst yet in a state of probation, she shall be like the Church in heaven, so great will be her glory, her union, love, and peace.

After the closing conflict of rationalism the next

period will be entered on; and it is for this crisis that we see the Church burnishing her armour, and rousing her children. May the Cistercian Order not be found wanting, when called upon to do her part of the work assigned her. Each Order has its peculiar spirit and mission. For the end and aim of every Order is to exhibit a living embodiment of certain features of the Evangelical Counsels.

An Order fulfils its mission, in proportion as it keeps close to the spirit of its primitive institution. When it departs from the first principles of its foundation, it cannot accomplish its proper work; and its own decay and dissolution, are the result of its infidelity. If it jealously retains, and guards against infringement, the rules laid down by its Fathers; this is the gage of its prosperity and perpetuity.

May the Blessed Robert look down from heaven, and by his powerful prayers obtain, that, a second time, the Cistercian Order may spread itself through every nook and corner of his beloved England; and that in every land in the Church of the Future, her peculiar spirit may be perpetuated, as one of the most beautiful features of the Bride,—the Church of the living God.

LIFE OF S. ROBERT OF KNARESBROUGH.

CHAPTER I.

ROBERT'S CHILDHOOD—HE JOINS THE CISTERCIAN ORDER.

" Come while the blossoms of thy years are brightest,
Thou youthful wanderer in a flowery May;
Come while thy restless heart is bounding lightest,
And joy's pure sunbeams dazzle on thy way.
Life has but shadows, save a promise given,
Which lights the future with a fadeless ray.
Oh! touch the sceptre; win a hope in heaven:
Come! turn thy spirit from the world away."

ONE of the most striking characteristics of the present century, is the taste for Archæology. We delve into the past, that we may have exposed before our eyes its hidden treasures. The long buried labours of the Ninivetic sculptor are exhumed, and brought across sea and land, to satisfy our aching thirst. The Pyramidical sepulchres must give up their dead. The Catacombs of ancient Rome must reveal their secrets. The Rocks of the desert of Sinai must tell us what took place there, during the sojourn amongst them of God's chosen people. We would fain, if it were possible, procure some memorials of the state of mankind before the Deluge. We would like to have some monuments of the history of the people of those early days of the world's chronicles.

But the search of the Christian is, most of all, directed towards what have been called the Middle Ages; or, as some have been pleased to term them, the dark ages;—those ages which seem so full of obscurity;—covered from our eyes with a dark mysterious veil;—those ages, looked upon by some as ages of gross ignorance and superstition, when the lamp of Christianity was well-nigh gone out;—ages so unlike our own. Into these ages many, tempted by one motive or another, have made an experimental search, and have returned from it, with ideas very different from those with which they began the scrutiny. Indeed with all our boasted enlightenment, we have been forced to confess, that, in some points, we stand far inferior to the men of that period, which had been lost to our gaze, in the shadow that hung over it.

There were giants in those days;—men of intellect and a vast extent of knowledge, such as are not to be found anywhere, in our degenerate times. There were men who, in philosophic lore, attained heights and depths, such as had never entered into our imagination. We had no idea that men of such gifts and talents had ever existed; still less did we expect to find them in the dark ages. When we compare our knowledge with theirs, we become like Daniel in the presence of the Angel of God, "all our comeliness is changed into corruption." We find that we are but as grasshoppers in their presence; and all our high thoughts of the intellectual advancement of our own days are suddenly abashed, and brought low. We see that though knowledge in mediocrity is more common, and its circle more widely extended, yet we have no men of stature, that can bear comparison with the intellectual giants of those days.

Some of the philosophers of the present day have brought forth these great lights of the Middle Ages from their obscurity; and have ably shown that the contempt, accorded by ignorance to men of such high stamp, is utterly out of place. As ignorance is unable to appreciate the refined subtilties of wisdom, and treats them with contempt, so impiety is incapable of appreciating the high flights of exalted holiness. It is for this reason that the actions of the Saints appear, to the eyes of some, to be oftentimes vain, foolish, or even superstitious; and the incredulous esteem that to be a pious fable, which has any thing in it of an extraordinary character. But as the intellectual stars of the Middle Ages are now beginning to receive their due honour; it may be hoped that those saintly characters, which adorned the same epoch, will likewise have restored to them the veneration, and esteem, they so justly merit.

We are but now emerging from that scepticism, and indifference, which, during the last century, has infected, with a wasting blight, all the nations of Europe. It is difficult at once to repudiate ideas and notions, which so lately held under their sway even the highest intelligences. It is difficult to emancipate ourselves altogether from the slavery of those prejudices, which held our fathers so fast enchained. We may have detected their absurdity;—we may see how unfounded they were;—but still we do not like to be completely shorn of them ourselves. There seems a certain disrespect to our forefathers, in relinquishing even their false notions. We would therefore that these notions should die an easy and a natural death. We would have them to be buried with an honourable funeral.

False views of things can never live eternally. Their duration may be long, but they cannot hold out for ever against truth. Time, the avenger, renders at last to all their due. It is not then to be wondered at, that, with the restoration of the beauties of medieval art, a truer notion is beginning to prevail, concerning the great and holy men, who adorned that period of England's history; of whom S. Robert of Knaresbrough was one. A more perfect account of the life and character of this extraordinary man, than has hitherto been presented before the public eye, can hardly fail to be interesting to those, who are acquainted with his name, or who have beheld those monuments of himself, which he has left behind him.

About the year of our Blessed Lord, 1159, this Saint was born in the ancient City of York, when Roger, surnamed the good, who built the famous choir of the Cathedral, was Archbishop of the See, whilst Savaric presided, as fourth Abbot, over the Monastery dedicated to the Blessed Virgin, Mother of God. His father's name is by some authors given as Tockless or Took Floure, who was Lord Mayor of York, in the year 1195; and also a second time later on in the reign of Richard Cœur de Lion. By others, however, the surname of S. Robert is said to have been Coke, or de Cokcliff. Thus is there an apparent difficulty as to what his real family was. It must be remembered, however, that in those days, surnames were not of the fixed nature, which they have acquired in our own times. Many persons even took for a surname the town or village from whence they came. In the life of William of Wickham, we find that the dissimilar names of Perrot and Long are given by different authors of his life, as the surname of his parents; whilst for himself he had none but that of his village. The mother of S. Robert was called Semenia, and was of a respectable family. She had a great reputation for piety, and trained her children, from their very infancy, to the love and worship of God. Robert, who was her first-born, drank in eagerly all the holy lessons, which she inculcated upon his yet infantine mind; and the graces then received became again the seed of that plentiful harvest, which, in its hundredfold return, was reaped by God from his soul in after years. For that Robert was able, in later life, to scale those heights of perfection, to which he ultimately attained, is to be attributed to God's preventing grace, which, taking possession of his heart in early boyhood, prepared his feet by degrees for the dangerous pathway; God, according to the words of the psalmist, making his feet like hart's feet, and setting him up on high. Even when a boy, he took no pleasure in the clamorous mirth of childish sports,—in jumping, running, wrestling, and such like amusements; for the noise and tumult disturbed that peace and quiet, with which his tranquil soul had been filled by God. He therefore avoided all these things, and would retire secretly, to clasp his little hands in prayer, turning his upward gaze to heaven; from whence alone he desired to receive all his joy and consolation.

Robert then abstained from the noisy mirth of childish games; not because such mirth is in itself sinful, but because by a particular vocation of God, he was called, even when a child, to put away childish things. For that this sort of play, though allowable and even profitable to many, is out of place in those predetermined by God to great sanctity, may be gathered from what happened to the Venerable Cuthbert, when he was yet a child. Of him it is related, that, up to his eighth year, he joined with great glee in childish games; and, when he had tired out all his playmates, would stand, and look about with proud eye, seeing that none was able to cope with him. But one day, when in boyish fun, he and his young companions began to twist their bodies into various unnatural forms; on a sudden a little boy, only three years old, ran to him, and besought him to desist. But the young Cuthbert paying no heed, the little boy began to cry piteously. Cuthbert, surprised, tried to comfort him, but in vain; when on a sudden, looking up in his face he said: "Why do you, Cuthbert, holy priest and bishop, do things so unbecoming your high character and rank? when the Lord has consecrated you to be a teacher of the ancients, it does not befit you to be following the sports of children."

After this admonition Cuthbert put away childish things, and became more grave and sober.

In like manner, by interior drawings the Holy Spirit withdrew the blessed Robert from the company of his equals in age. For the very beginning of his history is sanctified by the prophet Jeremias, when in exaltation of the perfection of a hermit's mode of life, he says: "It is good for a man, when he hath borne the yoke from his youth ; he shall sit solitary and shall be silent, for he shall raise himself above himself." Hungering after the sweetness of so excellent a thing, Robert bent his neck early beneath the yoke of divine discipline. He rejoiced to sit solitary ; and, lest the sound of men's voices should cause him to lose something of the divine colloquies of the heavenly Spirit, he was willing even to be silent from good words. His youthful piety was of so marked a character, that his parents, being persuaded that he had a vocation for the Ecclesiastical State, procured for him a learned education.

In the Middle Ages those who were brought up to arms or commerce, or to serve other offices in the state, took little pains to learn letters. Those who were not intended for the Sacred Ministry were content, for the most part, to be taught their Christian duties by their parish priest. They esteemed reading and writing to be things quite superfluous, and beyond the requirements of their calling. Robert had a great love of learning ; and his unaffected piety was such as to draw on him the eyes of all; for it was evident, from the spotless purity of his life, that the Lord was with him in an especial manner. Having passed through the minor Orders, he was, at length, ordained Sub-deacon, being thus irrevocably given to God for the Ecclesiastical State. Some little time after this, he determined to go and pay a visit to a younger brother of his, who had embraced the Cistercian Rule at the Abbey of Newminster in Northumberland. Although the fervour of this Order was not altogether such as it had been at its first institution, yet the life of the Monks was still most strict and holy. Robert was so charmed with the manner of their devotion, innocency, and all their behaviour, that he became one of them, being invested in the white habit of their Noviciate. He continued with them fourteen weeks; at the end of which, discovering that his vocation was not that of a Cistercian Monk, he determined on returning home for a time, till he should see what God might wish to do with him. He accordingly took a kind farewell of his brother; and, to the regret of the whole Community, went back to the house of his parents at York.

CHAPTER II.

ROBERT TURNS HERMIT—HIS CAVE AND CHAPEL AT KNARESBROUGH.

> *"And now, attended by their host,*
> *The Hermitage they viewed,*
> *Deep hewn within a craggy cliff,*
> *And overhung with wood.*
> *And near a flight of shapely steps,*
> *All cut with nicest skill,—*
> *And, piercing through a stony arch,*
> *Ran winding up the hill."*
> —HERMIT OF WARKWORTH.

ROBERT did not remain long at home on his return from Newminster. It is not unlikely that, before his return, he had made up his mind as to what should be his future course of life, and only waited the desired opportunity of putting himself under some one's direction. God's providence seemed to favour him in this point; for he received the report of one who lived an anchorite's life amongst the cliffs which are to be found on the outskirts of Knaresbrough. He determined to go and place himself under the guidance of this man, that, instructed by his lessons, and by his life, he might learn how afterwards to battle with the Enemy of souls, in the single combat of a life of complete solitude.

There seems no reason to suppose that his parents were opposed to his vocation, although it is said that he left them secretly. He did this, doubtless, from the promptings of an affectionate heart, which could not bear to encounter the tears of a tender mother, or the prolonged pains of leave-taking. He therefore with a sharp stroke cut the tie by a secret flight. His parents were not of those who, whilst they recognise, as a matter of faith, that a call to Religion is a privilege, yet in action throw hindrances in the way to keep their children from embracing that call.

There was a something more precious to them, than to have continually with them the bodily presence of their beloved son. Some parents desire for their sons that they may become great in worldly estate;—that they may obtain wealth, high rank, power, and rule;—that they may be men of fame, and mix among the nobles of the land. But such paltry desires were not those of the parents of Robert. They had for him a higher ambition,—that of seeing him exalted to be one of the favourites of the King of Heaven. To keep their son from promotion to so high an honour, from an over-fond attachment to his bodily presence, would have been a heartless selfishness, of which true love could never be guilty. Proud, therefore, of their son's advancement in the excellent glory and beauty of holiness, they parted with him; and the thought of the exalted life of their son was a loadstone, which, whilst it drew them to him, at the same time loosened the ties of all earthly things, and prepared their hearts for heaven.

Knaresbrough is about eighteen miles from York. The sorrows of an affectionate heart no doubt mingled with the higher aspirations of our Saint, as he left his beloved home, and took his path leading to this town. Knaresbrough was then surrounded by a dense forest, over which frowned the strong castle of the Lord Estoteville.

The river Nidd, flowing from the bare uplands of the Great Whernside hill over limestone steppes, and through wild moor country, passes on through various village-hamlets, till, nearing Knaresbrough, its banks become steep and rugged, and below the town tall cliffs, like those of our southern coast, rise precipitous on its sides.

To one who comes from York, after crossing a bridge, beneath which the water glides swift and clear, the banks, hitherto flat and unseemly, become broken; and on the right of the stream a rough rock shoots up from the green turf, called after the sainted hermit Grimbald Crag. Thence pleasant woods, and sloping banks, stretch with many a bend past the town of Knaresbrough.

Nearly opposite the crag, half concealed in a leafy bower, is a low dark cliff; and at the bottom, reached by a rudely-constructed stair, is a small cave, partly the work of nature, and partly hewn by the hand of man. The roof of it is covered with rude carvings of crosses, initials of names, and other things. At the farthest part of it is a small recess, which seems to have served as a pantry. The places where the shelves have been fixed are yet evident. Above the entrance, on the front part of the rock, are traces of an upper apartment, the ascent to which was made by a small flight of steps, cut in the rock, part of which are yet discernible on the side of the rock next the bridge.

This seems to have been the place where S. Robert first began his eremitical life; but the man whom he took for his guide proved to be only a feigned hermit, and really one of the knights of King Richard's army, who, having deserted his post, was endeavouring to escape detection and pursuit through this deceit. He shortly after Robert's arrival thought it safe to resume his former occupations; and so returned to his wife and family.

In front of this cave, on a narrow platform of rock, are still to be seen the foundations of a small Chapel. The altar steps and walls, the buttresses, and the stairs leading down to the river, are all plainly visible.

At the foot of the altar steps is the grave of S. Robert, —sunk deep in the living rock.

No hermit's cell could be better chosen. This was the Chapel of the Holy Cross, built by Walter the brother of the blessed Robert; and here it was that for more than two hundred years lay all that remained of the sainted man. The marble slab on one of the tombs of the Slingsbys in Knaresbrough Church, which is said to have come from the tomb of S. Robert, is supposed now rather to have been taken from some tomb in Knaresbrough Priory, and not from that of the Saint, to which it is disproportioned.

Devout persons are interested in beholding S. Robert's cave, because it is sanctified by having been once the earthly dwelling-place of this holy anchorite. It was here he raised his pure hands in prayer to God. Here fell his tears of compunction. Here on his hard stone bed, hewn with his own hand out of the living rock, he took his scanty yet calm repose. But this cave has another claim to interest of a totally different nature: it is this, that Eugene Aram, the murderer, a schoolmaster at Knaresbrough, and a man of great learning, hid here the body of Adam Clarke whom he had killed, and which was discovered fourteen years afterwards. What conflicting sentiments are there not raised in the mind of the beholder, on being made acquainted with this circumstance! How utterly unsuited for such a scene of crime was the peaceful hermit's cell!

Down below Grimbald Bridge is S. Robert's well, a spring of very cold water which runs into the river. The access to it is closed up with bushes; but its virtue has not been altogether forgotten; and, no long time back, it was customary for persons to bathe in the waters issuing from it, for the sake of their healthful influence.

Not far from S. Robert's cave, as the ascent is made up the river, are to be seen, after an entombment of three hundred years, some foundations, which tell of the ancient Priory of the Order of the Holy Trinity. This Order occupied itself in obtaining alms, for the redemption of captives from Mahometan slavery. The whole of S. Robert's lands were, shortly after his death, made over to this Order. It would appear that Ivo, who after his death was made Superior of the Robertine Brotherhood, was not capable of sustaining so great a task. Still further on up the river, whose rising green banks, sheltered by the high precipitous cliffs, are topped with towering trees, is to be found the Chapel of S. Giles, now called S. Robert's Chapel. Its length is about ten feet by nine in width, and seven and a half in height. The decoration of the Chapel is later than the time of S. Robert; the roof being groined and the altar carved. Here the holy Sacrifice was no doubt offered; as the altar, being covered with little crosses, bears marks of its having been consecrated. Anciently a small cross was made wherever on the altar a drop of the holy oil had fallen. There are also at the corners, and in the centre of the forepart of the altar, little pits, in which were bestowed the relics of the Saints, thus united with the altar; no altar being consecrated without relics.

In the centre of the floor there is a hollow, which may have contained some portion of the relics of the Saint, or perhaps some brass memorial. On the right hand side, cut upon the wall, are four faces; three are grouped together; the fourth appears to have been added by another hand; some persons have imagined them to be an allusion to the Holy Trinity. Medieval art does not countenance such a supposition. They were most probably an attempt at ornament made by one of the friars.

Outside the Chapel, and, as it were, guarding the entrance, is the figure of an armed man, cut in the living rock. This appears to have been made as a commemoration of the vision which was seen by the Lord Estoteville; as afterwards to be related.

The whole of the Chapel is cut out of the living rock; having an arched doorway, and a mullioned window. These things being now related, the history of S. Robert may be pursued with more of interest.

CHAPTER III.

ROBERT'S WAY OF LIFE—HE GOES TO SPOFFORTH—
HIS VISION AND RETURN TO KNARESBROUGH.

> "*There are the naked clothed, the hungry fed,*
> *And charity extendeth to the dead.*
> *Her intercessions, made for the soul's rest*
> *Of tardy penitents; or for the best*
> *Amongst the good (when love might else have slept,*
> *Sickened, or died;) in pious memory kept.*"

THE beginning of Robert's eremitical life must certainly have been very hard to flesh and blood. Custom and the companionship of those we love, will render the most dreary life tolerable; but Robert was early left alone, without any previous training, to a life of solitude, and all unaccustomed to its hardships.

If, however, he had received no training on the part of man, there was given to him a much more excellent and efficacious one from the hands of God; which consisted in a total separation of the heart from all affection to created things. Through this holy disposition of soul, the very destitution of all things, in which he found himself, affected him with keen delight. Poverty, which to the carnal eye presents so revolting an appearance, has an altogether different aspect, when regarded with the light of faith. By that light it is seen to be full of divine charms; for when the Son of God espoused it to Himself in the manger of Bethlehem, He took away from it all natural hideousness, clothing instead with His robe of glory. For those who should voluntarily make choice of it, He exalted it to a sublime state of perfection, endowing its profession with His highest supernatural graces.

Thus poverty has become ennobled, and as it were deified; because the Eternal Word has deigned to be born, to live, and die, in the condition of a poor man;—at one time supported by the labour of His hands, at another by the free-will offerings of His faithful—Robert, with an illuminated eye, beheld the splendour of this holy poverty, and embraced it with eager mind. It was for this he had left father and mother, house and lands, which he would have inherited as his father's first-born. He left all these things, and counted them as dung and dross, that he might find Christ, and be found in Him, a true disciple and lively copy of His ways and spirit. He sighed not for the comforts of his paternal home; but counted the poverty of Christ more precious than all the treasures of the Egypt he had left. After having lived some time amongst the Cliffs at Knaresbrough,

Robert changed his place of abode to the neighbourhood of Spofforth. For the supply of his necessities, or those of the poor he entertained, he had been begging an alms of a rich matron, who lived not far distant from thence. She, admiring his holy conversation, offered for his use a little chapel dedicated to S. Hilda, and with it as much land as he should be able to cultivate. This place still goes by the name of Hile's Nook; but the ruined buildings were not long since removed in order to be used as materials for the construction of the Church of S. Mary's at Knaresbrough. The Saint accepted the kind offer of his benefactress, who is supposed to have been a lady of the ancient family of the Percies, whose seat was at Spofforth.

Some lawless men, however, after he had been there about a year, having no respect to his sanctity, broke into his cell one night, and robbed him of all his store; so that, dreading the dangers of his unprotected solitude, and being without provisions, he removed to the village of Spofforth. Here, however, he encountered another evil; for a great concourse of people daily besieged him for the benefit of his advice and counsel in their spiritual maladies. His words gave light and fire to their souls, dissipating doubts and difficulties, and kindling into fervour their cold or tepid hearts. He was meditating as to where he might retire to, when the Monks of Hedley, a Cell of the Benedictine Order, in the parish of Bramham, sent a messenger to him, inviting him to come and take up his abode with them. He gladly took advantage of this offer; seeking thereby to shun the glory which men gave him, and hoping in this Brotherhood to lead quietly a strict and severe life, without being noticed for his sanctity. But the austerity of his life was not liked by the looser sort of the Brethren; being esteemed by them a kind of reproach to their relaxation. They led him, therefore, no pleasant life, being impatient of his rebukes.

Perceiving that he was now an unwelcome guest, he returned to the Chapel of S. Hilda, where he was joyfully received by his patroness. She presently set on workmen, who built him a safer place for the storing of his corn, and for other necessary uses.

Being now more at ease, he gave himself up to a life of asceticism and prayer, spending whole nights sometimes in that holy exercise. When he slept, which was but little, he made the bare ground his bed. His garment, for he had but one, was of a white colour, but so thin as to serve him rather as a cover for his nakedness, than a protection against the cold. His bread was mostly of coarse barley meal. This he ate with a broth made of unsavoury herbs; or he had served for him a few beans seasoned with salt, and once a-week a little meal was mixed with it to give it a relish.

Being now established on what he thought a secure footing, he took certain others into his company.

He Goes to Spofforth.

Two were employed in the more arduous labours of tillage, a third in various matters, and a fourth used to go abroad to beg for his Community, and for the alms which he distributed to the poor. Robert, however, used also himself to labour in the tillage of the ground.

One day it chanced that, as he slept upon the grass, wearied out with his work, his mother, being lately dead, appeared to him very sad, pale, and disfigured. She told him that, though in some sort she had lived a pious life, yet for usury, and divers other transgressions, she was condemned to most grievous pains, unless he relieved her by the efficacy of his prayers. Being much troubled for the discomfort of his mother, he willingly promised to aid her all he could; and accordingly applied himself to prayer in her behalf; whereupon shortly afterwards she appeared to him again with a cheerful, shining countenance; and giving thanks to her son, she in his sight glided up on high, with a hymn of praise. Thus, by his law of mutual dependence, God cuts away the root of egotism; for no one lives for himself alone. Even after death the bond of charity is still in force, for even the dead can be assisted by, and can assist, the living. Such has ever been the consoling belief of Christianity.

In the annals of the early Church there is recorded in the life of S. Perpetua, the martyr, a circumstance similar to that which has just been narrated of S.

Robert. Whilst in prison for the faith, she had a revelation concerning the fate of her companions, which was fulfilled in all its circumstances a few days afterwards. Soon after she had a second vision. She had been praying for her departed brother, Dynocrates, when the following night she sees him come from a darksome place with many others. He appeared devoured with thirst; his face being disfigured by a cancer, of which he had died. Between him and her was a great space, which prevented their coming near each other. In the place where he stood was a cistern, but the margin was too high for him to be able to reach the water. He stretched himself as if to drink, and S. Perpetua woke. She comprehends from this that her brother is suffering; and she hopes to obtain relief by her prayers. She prays night and day, with abundance of tears. She has another vision. The body of her brother is clean and well-clad. There is on his face but a slight scar. The border of the cistern is lower; he takes a cup that lies by the side of the spring, and drinks. He leaves the water and begins playing with other children: S. Perpetua understands that he no longer suffers. Such is the relation of the great S. Augustine, who supposes the boy, only seven years old, had been guilty of some faults, for which he suffered some temporary pains.

It might have been expected that Robert, under the care of his patroness, would have remained now in undisturbed possession of S. Hilda's Chapel, and the building she had erected for his use. Matters, however, did not so turn out. The days in which he lived, were days in which many a lawless deed was committed; and had no avenger but the wrath of heaven. The feudal barons were like petty kings, who did much as they pleased, without fear of higher control. It chanced then that William Estoteville, Lord of the Forest, passing by the cell, demanded of his servants who lived there. They answered, "One Robert, a holy hermit." "No," answered he, "but rather a receiver of thieves;" and full of anger, he commanded his followers to level the whole to the ground, which was accordingly done; and Robert was left to shift for himself as well as he could. He, bearing the proud insult with Christian meekness, returned to the cliffs of Knaresbrough. Here he constructed a hut, made up principally of the boughs of trees, near what was then called the Chapel of S. Giles, but which is now called that of S. Robert. The sanctity of this man of God increased day by day; and by means of his word and bright example many were brought out of the kingdom of Satan to the practice of a holy life. This caused the Prince of darkness to make another attempt at his overthrow. The Lord Estoteville, passing that way, by the suggestion of the wicked one, took notice of the smoke, which curled up from the cell; whereupon he demanded presently who lived there. His servants answered him, "Robert the hermit." "Is it," said he, "that same Robert whom I not long since expelled from my Forest?" "The very same," his servants replied.

Then this instrument of the Devil swore, with a great oath, that on the next day he would drive Robert out of the place, and overthrow his hut to the ground. With these thoughts in his mind, he went to rest himself on his bed; when behold! in the middle of the night, there appeared to him, in a vision, three men terrible to behold. Two of them carried a burning engine, as big as the whole floor of his chamber, and spiked with sharp fiery teeth; whilst the third, a person of elegant form and stature, holding in his hands two large maces of iron, came to the bed, challenging him to fight with these words: "Now shalt thou know that no one is like the Lord in strength, whose servant thou wouldst persecute."

Upon beholding this fearful sight, the potent Lord trembled exceedingly; and, struck with terror and remorse of conscience, cried out to God for mercy; protesting that he repented sincerely of his wicked purpose, upon which the dreadful vision presently vanished. On awaking from sleep, he conceived great compunction of heart for the violence which he had formerly done to Robert, and for the evils he intended against him; taking the vision to be a merciful interference of God, to prevent his committing so heinous a thing. He therefore, to prove his altered mind, conferred on the servant of God all the lands between his cell and Grimbald Crag, for a perpetual alms; and that the ground might not lie untilled, he gave him, over and above, two oxen and two horses every year, and food for thirty poor men for twelve days after Christmas. He also ordered a granary to be built, and a house for the poor.

Thus by the good Providence of God, Robert only prospered the more on account of the machinations of the Devil, for what the Enemy contrived for his destruction became the cause of exaltation to honour.

CHAPTER IV.

ROBERT'S MIRACLES—VISIT OF KING JOHN—ROBERT'S DEATH AND BURIAL.

> "*A little lowly hermitage it was,*
> *Down in a dell, hard by a Forest side,*
> *Far from resort of people that did pass,*
> *In travaill to and fro; a little wyde*
> *There was a little Chapel edifyed;*
> *Wherein the Hermite daly went to say*
> *His holy things, each morn and even tyde;—*
> *Thereby a crystall streame did gently play,*
> *Which from a sacred fountaine welled forth away.*"
> —SPENSER'S "FAERYE QUEENE."

ROBERT being established now, took into his company one named Ivo, a holy man whose spirit of penance was so great that he walked barefoot in the coldest days in winter. Oftentimes his feet, sticking to the ice, became so wounded, that his footsteps might be traced along the road, by means of the blood which flowed from them. He used to go to York and other places, begging for the poor, for whom Robert's care was great.

It has before been said that Robert's habitation was a mere hut, constructed of the branches of trees; and though he was well contented in this poverty, others desired better lodging for him. Accordingly, when his brother Walter came from York to see him, he felt ashamed and grieved to see him in so miserable a habitation, and sending masons from York with timber and other requisites, they built for Robert the Chapel of the Holy Cross, with square stones, opposite to Grimbald Crag, and near to the cave, which the servant of God henceforth made his dwelling. Here a brotherhood was formed upon rules which the man of God ordained for them. Ivo before mentioned was the principal one. But this very man, one day overcome by a temptation of the Devil, thought to leave the company of the Saint. But as he was making haste in his flight, by a special providence, he got a severe fall, through which he broke his leg. Now, Robert, knowing by revelation the mishap that had overtaken him, went to him with speed, and chid him for his fault with all meekness. Ivo humbly acknowledged his error, and begged pardon of the man of God, who interceded for him with the Lord, blessed the leg, all imbrued with blood, and touching it with his holy hand restored it safe and sound. The repentant Brother, with great thankfulness, promised that he would never think to forsake his cell any more.

The sanctity of Robert was so great that even the

unreasoning animals felt its power, and became obedient to him. Once, when, for the wants of the poor he desired some further alms of his patron, there was given to him a certain cow so wild and fierce, that none dare come near her. But this blessed man, trusting in the divine assistance, went at once after her into the Forest, and having found her, he put his arm about her neck, and led her home as quiet as a lamb, to the great amazement of the spectators. Now one of the servants of the Lord Estoteville was filled with envy and indignation, at what he thought an injury to the property of his Master. He, therefore, determined to devise a means to get possession of the cow again; and though his master did not approve of it, he attempted to carry out his wicked plan, which was as follows: he went to Robert with counterfeit looks and gestures, feigning himself to be lame both of hands and feet; saying also that his wife and children were miserably oppressed with want, and in danger of starvation from hunger. With this piteous story he thought to deceive Robert: the holy man, however, saw through his wicked purpose; and therefore, whilst he allowed him to take the cow, he did so with this condition, that he should really become as lame as he made himself out to be. "God," said he, "gave and God shall have, but so as thou shall really be as thou feignest thyself to be." When, therefore, this deceiver wished to depart with the cow, he found himself of a sudden lame both of hands and feet, and quite unable to stir. Thus did God glorify His servant in the punishment of this hypocrite; for as Cicero says, "*Nihil est quod Deus efficere non possit, et quidem sine labore ullo.*" As much as to say, "There is nothing, however great and surprising, but what God can accomplish, either to punish the wicked or reward the just, and that without any difficulty whatsoever." This wretched man, seeing that the judgment of God had overtaken him, for attempting to play a trick upon His servant, cried out, "O Robert, true servant of God, pardon my trespass and the injury I have done you." The indulgent and good Father instantly forgave him; and having restored to him the use of his limbs, Robert returned into his cell.

Another instance of Robert's power over the brute creation, was formerly thought worthy of being commemorated in stained glass in the Church of the Holy Trinity at Knaresbrough. A company of deer from the Forest haunted his ground, doing much injury to his corn, and the other produce of his farm. Whereupon he complained to his patron, desiring of him that something might be done to restrain them. "Robert," answered the Lord Estoteville, "I give you free liberty to impound these deer, and to detain them till you are satisfied. The holy man, upon this permission, went into the fields, and with a little rod drove the deer out of the corn, like so many lambs, and shut them up in his barn. Having acquainted his patron with what he had done, he desired to know how he should further proceed. His patron gave him permission freely to use the deer he had so impounded in the plough, or in any other service of husbandry. Robert, returning many thanks, went home to his cell; and, taking the deer out of the barn, he put them under the yoke to plough his ground like oxen, which was daily seen and admired by all.

So it pleased God to reward the piety of His servant. For when Adam revolted from the obedience due to his Creator, the lower animals, which had formerly been subservient to him, shook off his yoke, and refused submission. But as Robert, on the contrary, had taken up again the sweet yoke, laid by Christ upon him, God in return made the lower creation subservient to his will.

After this the Lord Estoteville died; and was, for his beneficent deeds, buried in the Chapel at Fountains Abbey. All his possessions were made over by King John to the Lord Bryan de Lisle. This man, loving Robert much, often made mention of him to the great nobles of the court; and when King John came into the north to hunt, he was persuaded by him to visit Robert. The king, therefore, came with a great concourse of people to the humble cell of the man of God. Robert, however, remained prostrate in prayer, paying no attention, till the Lord Bryan went up to him, and said to him secretly: "Rise, Brother Robert, the king is come, desirous to see thee."

Then he arose; and taking an ear of corn from the floor, said to King John: "If you are a king, make an ear such as this;" which the king in reply acknowledged himself unable to do. "There is no king then," answered Robert, "but the Lord only." Robert so spoke, not out of rudeness, but to bring down the overbearing pride of the kings of those days, by showing that, after all, they were but men. It was thus that S. Antony treated Constantine the Great and his son Constantius. He did not at once answer the letters they sent, but making little account of such an honour, he told his disciples that they were not to think it much, that an Emperor, a mere mortal, should write to him; but rather ought to admire, that the eternal God had been so good as not only to write His law for men, but had sent His Son to visit them.

John, hard to others, was softened: he was not offended with this want of ceremony on the part of Robert, but pleased. He, therefore, conferred on him as much of his waste wood adjoining as he could convert into tillage, with one plough or team, for the service of the poor. He gave him also free liberty to cut the trees or brushwood for bedding.

Robert had also the gift of prophecy, by which he foretold to Lord Bryan de Lisle, who came for his benediction, the good success of a voyage he was to make on the king's business, adding, however, that he should never return. He foretold also that the Rector of Knaresbrough, a well learned man, but covetous, should come to a miserable end, because with violence he exacted tithes of the land; thereby robbing God's poor of a part of their heritage.

This clergyman shortly afterwards became mad; and without making his confession, or receiving the holy sacraments, died; crying and howling, and biting his tongue. Thus was given a terrible warning to those, who would afflict the servants of God. And as he died without making a will, the king's myrmidon's seized his goods.

When Robert was drawing near his end, he sent for a priest to prepare him for death; and fortified himself by receiving the holy Viaticum. The Monks of Fountains Abbey hearing of it, sent some of their company, to try and prevail on him to be invested with the habit of their Order. This they did with the intention of claiming his corpse as that of a Cistercian Monk. Robert, however, humbly excused himself; saying that his own robe, which he usually wore, was quite enough for him, and he desired no other. Having it revealed to him that they would try to carry off his body when dead, he certified the same to the Brethren; and advised them to get armed assistance to resist such an endeavour. Ivo and the rest of his company gathered weeping round their Father, as he lay in his mortal agony, and desiring of him his last blessing. Whilst he lifted up his hand over them to give them a benediction, he yielded up his blessed spirit. It being noised abroad that he was dead, the Monks of Fountains again came, bringing the habit of their Order, in which they invested the remains of the holy man; and then attempted to carry them off by violence, but a band of armed men from the Castle resisted them, and they were compelled to retire in sorrow at losing so great a treasure.

This proceeding of getting possession of the relics of a Saint, by craft or force, was no unusual one in those days, but quite according to the spirit of the times.

Thus we read, that when the holy hermit Henry of the Island of Cocket in Northumberland died, the Benedictine Monks of Tynemouth hastened to the Island to carry off the body, and bury it in their own Church. The people of the neighbouring parish put to sea in boats to resist them. They were no sooner at sea, however, than they found themselves enveloped in a thick mist as black as night. Thus they lost their way; and meantime the Monks with their holy lading arrived safely at Tynemouth, and buried the body near that of S. Oswin in an arch of the wall on the south side of the Church.

The Monks of Fountains were not so fortunate, but returned home defeated. Then the body of S. Robert was laid in his Chapel of the Holy Cross in a new tomb. Great multitudes of people came to pay him these last honours, kissing with deep devotion the coffin wherein his body was enclosed. Like the body of the prophet Eliseus, so the body of Robert wrought miracles after his death; a sweet smelling medicinal oil, issuing forth abundantly from the body, by which many maladies were cured. This testimony is given of him by the Benedictine Monk, Matthew of Paris.

The expression of dying in the odour of sanctity, has no doubt its origin in the fact, that after death many bodies of the Saints, instead of emitting an odour of corruption, have, on the contrary, like that of S. Robert, sent forth the most delicious perfume.

In all these cases death found in the body a predisposition for the formation of this oil, which only developed itself more or less rapidly.

It was on September 24, in the year of our Lord 1218, that Robert died, as is testified by the Chronicles of Lanercost Priory. Isaias says of Jesus Christ, "His sepulchre shall be glorious." So it is with His Saints. They live in abjection, and are buried in glory. The aristocracy of holiness, by God's decree, lifts a man above kings, and his name is held in honour, when the very remembrance of the great ones of the earth has perished. The death of this poor man Robert was esteemed a public calamity. The only comfort the people of Knaresbrough had was, that his blessed relics remained with them. As they prayed by his tomb they hoped that his intercession might be offered for them before God, with whom the prayers of the righteous man avail much.

The ancient Church of Pannal, and a recent one at Harrogate, are dedicated under the Invocation of

S. Robert of Knaresbrough. Perhaps there may be others also under his patronage in the neighbourhood.

The present Church thus resumes its bond with that of the past, and repairs the link, broken by the lawless tyranny of Henry VIII. It was by the sacrilegious hands of this prince that Knaresbrough Priory was demolished, and its revenues confiscated. The Chapel of the Holy Cross was plundered no doubt at the same time. The body of S. Robert lay there enshrined, and very probably still incorrupt, as is the case with the bodies of several of the Saints at this present day, for instance, that of S. Catharine of Sienna. It would meet, however, with but little reverence from these fanatical and irreligious men, who took a malicious delight in showing scorn for all that is holy. In the excavations that have been made no trace has been discovered of it. Perhaps these rude men threw it into the river flowing by. As religion waned in the hearts of the people, the respect felt for S. Robert died away, so that a few years back his Chapel, consecrated by his prayers and tears, and the offering of the Holy Sacrifice, was used as a gardenhouse by a neighbouring cottager, and as a roost for hens. But a far better spirit is beginning now to prevail, with regard to holy persons and holy things. Efforts are being made on all sides to raise religion from that ruin into which it fell in the days of Henry VIII. Already we see the ancient fanes being everywhere reconstructed, or restored, in their primitive beauty and splendour; whilst new edifices, built after the old types and models of Christian art, rise by their side. These buildings are the expression of that revival of religious sentiment, which has made itself felt throughout the length and breadth of the land.

For it must not be supposed that the love of Christian types of art in contradistinction to those of paganism is a mere matter of taste. The appreciation of Christian art, whether in architecture, painting, music, or any other thing, betokens a certain temper and tone of mind, with which these things harmonise. It may not be easy to point out clearly the exact relationship between Christian art and Christian doctrine, yet there can be no doubt a relationship does exist between them, and that they exercise mutually an influence, one over the other, the perfection of the one inducing the perfection of the other. Over and above the teaching of the actual emblems and symbolical signs so closely interwoven with all Christian art, its effect generally is to elevate the mind above earth and lead it to the supernatural.

At present S. Robert's Chapel is visited merely as a venerated relic of old times. The day, however, may not be far distant when it shall be restored by some kindly hand, and reconverted to its ancient uses.

www.ingramcontent.com/pod-product-compliance
Lightning Source LLC
Chambersburg PA
CBHW020905230426
43666CB00008B/1325